More
than can be
Measured

by Rona Swanson

First published by CrossBooks 10/30/2012

Library of Congress Control Number: 2012920315

This book is printed on acid-free paper.

Any people depicted in stock imagery provided by Thinkstock are models, and such images are being used for illustrative purposes only.

Certain stock imagery © Thinkstock.

Because of the dynamic nature of the Internet, any web addresses or links contained in this book may have changed since publication and may no longer be valid. The views expressed in this work are solely those of the author and do not necessarily reflect the views of the publisher, and the publisher hereby disclaims any responsibility for them.

Dedication

This book is dedicated to all who have attempted
to pursue love fully, with their whole heart.

It is not without great risk.

Our hearts can be broken and smashed in ways
more painful and ruinous than we could have imagined.

This is my story of loss deeper than the deepest pit...
and love that pulled me out.

Table of Contents

Prelude 1

1. A Call in the Night 3

2. Alone with Grief 6

3. Chilled to the Bone 9

4. News No One Wants to Hear 13

5. The Longest Journey 15

6. Big Sis 19

7. Un-niceties 23

8. News and Photo Albums 27

9. Who's to Know? 30

10. Making Arrangements 33

11. Plotting Together 37

12. Sweet Voices 41

13. E-notification and Reluctant Cleansing 43

14. Demands 45

15. Precious in the Sight of the Lord 47

16. Shiva 49

17. A Weary Stand 53

18. Crowded Home 58

19. From Paralytic to Carrying My Own Stretcher 61

20. A Celebration of Life 65

21. Food 71

22. Descent into Darkness 73

23. Our Reasonable Worship 77

24. A Holiday 79

25. Gray and Gentle Day 83

26. The Burial 85

27. Coming to Grips 89

Table of Contents
(continued)

28.   Lost in Memories 93

29.   Try to Return 99

30.   Back to Work 101

31.   Computer 103

32.   Back to School 107

33.   Invitation 111

34.   Gone Gray 117

35.   Doing Well? 120

36.   Daniel 125

37.   Wedding Announcement 131

38.   Easter 134

39.   Accident Report 137

40.   Pinning Ceremony 142

41.   Mother's Day 147

42.   Media Contact 151

43.   Wedding Day 156

44.   Memorial Day 162

45.   Funeral 165

46.   Writing Contest 169

47.   Family Reunion 171

48.   Election Season and See How They Run 178

49.   Thanksgiving 180

50.   Christmas 185

51.   Yahrzeit 191

52.   Where Do We Go From Here? 196

53.   Afterword 198

Aknowledgements 203

Preface

There are moments in life that change us forever.

I know I am not the only one who has ever experienced loss.

I am not the only one who has ever gone through pain.

But this is my story.

Unlike the disclaimers on so many messages, I will tell you that these events are true and happened to me.

I have woven my daughter's voice with mine throughout the story, taken from her journals and other writings.

Our hearts were so tenderly bound to one another that in that one moment, like entwined roots ripped from fertile soil, I think a tiny bit of my own heart passed right into eternity with her.

Will you take my hand and come on this journey together with me?

We will walk through dark valleys, but we will not walk alone.

– Rona Swanson, Feb. 4, 2012

More

than can be

Measured

Prelude

It began as a game.

"Mommy, how much do you love me?'

"So, SOOO much!"

"Higher than the rope-swing oak tree?"

"Much, much higher!"

"Bigger than a big tall mountain?"

"Much, much bigger!"

"Farther than the moon?"

"Much, much farther! Beyond the farthest, farthest star and then beyond it!"

"Wider than the ocean?"

"Much, much wider!"

"Deeper than the Grand Canyon?"

"WAY deeper!"

And then finally I had the answer...and it made perfect sense to both of us.

"Mommy, how much do you love me?'

"More than can be measured, my love, more than can be measured!"

It became a tagline to notes and e-mails and telephone sign-offs when she was older.

More, so much more than can be measured.

My daughter Rebekah playing
on the "rope-swing oak tree."

Rebekah on the carousel at Disneyland.

A Call in the Night

The phone is ringing. The room is pitch dark. I stumble to pick it up, noticing that the time is a little after 2 a.m.

"Hello."

"Is this Rona Swanson?"

"Yes."

"There is a policeman at your door."

"Excuse me?"

"This is the Visalia Police Department. There is a policeman at your door. Didn't you hear him?"

"No. I was asleep. Let me just look out the window and see if he is at our home."

I walked to the window and peeked down through the blinds from our second story bedroom. Sure enough, I could see a black and white cruiser parked in our driveway. I picked up the phone again. "Yes, I can see his car," I said. "I will go downstairs and answer the door."

Pulling on jeans and a shirt, I ran down the stairs and opened the front door for the officer standing there, inviting him in.

"Are you alone?" he asked.

I looked up at him, a bit confused. "No," I said.

"Who else is here?" he asked.

If anyone other than a police officer was asking this, I thought... but answered, "My husband is upstairs."

"Go get him," the officer instructed.

I went up the stairs to get my husband Sam. He was already awake and I explained that there was a police officer downstairs wanting to talk to us. We both went back downstairs and the officer stood and faced us.

"I have very bad news," he said, drawing a deep breath. "This is the hardest part of my job."

I smiled encouragement to him as he drew himself up to speak.

"I have very bad news," he repeated.

I nodded at him to continue.

"Are you Rona Swanson?" he asked me.

"I am."

"Do you have a daughter named Rebekah Swanson?"

I could hear my heart...thump, thump, thump as I answered, "I do."

Time slowed. The officer's eyes showed pain as he opened his mouth. My own heart was pounding, making my body feel its throb. The officer licked his lips and continued, "Rebekah was in an auto accident tonight," he said, "and she did not survive."

Sam made a sound as if he had received a physical blow and I saw him staggering to the couch, holding his chest. Sam had suffered a heart attack seven years before.

"Lord," I prayed, "don't let me lose him too."

My own heart felt as if it had become a bird and it flew in fluttering panic into my head, its feathers flapping against my ears in an attempt to escape. I felt as if in a moment it would find an escape and just fly away. In some ways, I wanted it to, but I gently placed my hands over my ears to prevent it.

The officer came closer to me. "You will need to speak to the coroner," he said, leaning over my bowed head.

I began walking to the kitchen and grabbed the phone.

"I can dial it for you," he offered.

"I can do it," I whispered and he read the numbers out to me as I pressed the buttons.

"Coroner's office," a voice said.

"I am Rona Swanson. I am calling about my daughter, Rebekah Swanson."

"Yes, Mrs. Swanson," the coroner replied, his voice softening. "I need to inform you that Rebekah was southbound on Freeway 41 at the interchange to 180. She was on the ramp to 180 when, for an unknown reason, she went over the abutment to the freeway. The accident occurred at 23:43 PM on 1-13-04. The investigating officer is J Banta and the report # is 2004-01133. You can call 268-0109 during regular business hours with any other questions."

As the coroner spoke, stating facts that my mind could not comprehend, I was scribbling the words on a piece of paper, knowing I would need every bit of assistance I could get to remember what was expected of me in the hours to come. We finished our conversation and the officer followed me back in to the living room where Sam came and stood beside me.

"Do you need me to get a chaplain?" the officer asked.

"No," Sam said gently. "We will call Pastor Guerra in the morning."

"That's First Assembly?" the officer asked and Sam nodded.

'My daughter goes to school there, that's a good church."

"Yes," Sam said. "We will contact them in the morning."

"Are you sure you will be okay?" the officer asked.

We nodded and I asked for the officer's name.

"Officer Lopez."

"Officer Lopez," I said. "I want to thank you for your kindness and compassion. A bright light has gone out in the universe tonight. You were a very brave man to bring this news to us, but I thank you for your kindness."

He stood looking at me and then asked, as we moved to the front door, "You're sure you will be okay?"

We smiled as he went out of the door and we closed it behind him.

❧ *Rebekah's Journal* ❧
Wait For Her

wait for an angel to come to you.
You will dance together
in the dark of the night
to the music of your heart.
She will bring you
through this hell
into the brightest of light.
Teaching you how to dance
in perfect time with your heart.

Alone with Grief

Sam and I went upstairs to our room. Once there, we wrapped our arms around each other, and stood leaned together as the tears began to flow.

"Dear God," I cried. "Dear God."

We clung to each other, writhing in pain. As we both gasped for breath, Sam sat down with his hands pressed together. His eyes were squeezed shut, yet tears were streaming down his cheeks. Suddenly, as if a dam had burst, sobs began to wrack his body. As I listened to his sorrow, my mind was flying back over a million memories and visions and glimpses of our precious daughter Rebekah.

Rebekah was twenty-one years old, a senior at Fresno Pacific University beginning her final semester, and the apple of my eye. Not one day passed without a phone call or a quick e-mail between the two of us. Even when she studied abroad in England during her junior year of college, we "talked" daily as I became proficient at the art of Instant Messaging on-line.

My heart cried out, desperate to race after Rebekah, to pursue her even as my mind was awakening to the fact that she was gone, far beyond my reach. I was in a free-fall into darkness. I sat, bent over, hugging myself with my arms, praying with all that was in me, Dear God, Dear God, Dear God. Time seemed to stand still as we cried out our sorrow.

As our sobs slowed to tortured breath, I kept hearing in my head the words, only love, only love...and prayed that God would help me, lead me, and guide me. I knew that only He would know the way out of this wasteland of loss. My eyes felt blinded by my sorrow. My heart shattered beyond repair.

"I need to call Jennifer and Jackie," I said. My credo was always that bad news can wait, but Rebekah's roommates at school would be worried if they woke up and she was not there. I called the number and Jennifer answered.

"Hello, Jen," I said. "I am sorry for waking you. I am so sorry to make this call but sweetheart, Rebekah was in an auto accident last night and she did not survive."

"No!" Jennifer cried.

"I am so sorry," I told her. "I am so sorry to have to tell you this, but I did not want you to hear it from anyone else or to wake up with Rebekah not there and be worried."

"Okay," she whispered.

"I will be in touch," I said.

"Okay," she said again.

"Will you be okay?" I asked.

"Yes," Jennifer replied. "Jackie is here, and we will call the others."

"Okay, I will talk to you later."

I stood frozen for a bit, staring at the phone, knowing the pain the phone had brought to that bright and adorable dorm room.

The phone rang and I picked it up.

"Hello?"

"Rona, it's Jen."

"Hello."

"Did you just call me?" she asked.

"Yes," I said. "Are you okay?"

"Yes, but I just wanted to make sure that it was you."

"I am sad to say, yes."

"Okay, I will let you go and I will talk to you later."

"Bye."

⟡ *Rebekah's Journal* ⟡

Heal Me

Please take my broken heart
into Your loving hands.
Mend it and bind it.
Touch the deepest part of me,
where only You can reach
and let me know that all will be well
when I have Your peace.

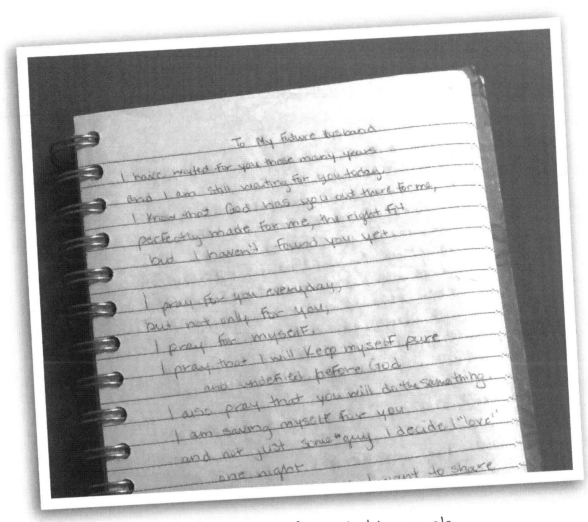

A page from one of Rebekah's journals.

Chilled to the Bone

I began to shake, chilled to the bone by the icy fingers of shock. All of my being wanted to argue with the harsh facts imparted to me by a coroner's office. I wanted to sleep and forget the dark news from the officer at our door. And yet I knew that I would need all of my wits about me as I prepared for a day like no other in my life because as soon as it was day, I would need to go to Rebekah's older brother and sister and tell them that their precious baby sis had passed away.

I ran a hot bath to combat the chills, and Sam and I called back to one another, random thoughts and memories and encouragement.

Then silence, each of us alone with our thoughts, and I remembered Rebekah, only a few days before. We were sitting in the living room and I watched her face dissolve into tears as she said, "Nobody loves me."

I hurried to her side, holding her close. "How can you say that?" I said. "EVERYONE loves you!"

"That's not what I mean," she explained. "I just don't have a special someone. I wonder if I will ever meet the man that I will marry."

I laughed at her then. Rebekah joked often about the fact that she planned to be the first Pentecostal Nun. She had lots of friends but no special guy friend, no one who she could see herself marrying.

As I remembered her tears and her longing, all of the conversations that we had had about her children, my grandbabies, and her wedding. "Just one little detail," she would always say, smacking her palm to her forehead, "the groom!"

"That will come, in God's time," I would reassure, confident that someone truly magnificent was out there, longing for her as well.

Now there would be no wedding, no sweet grandbabies that she and I would ooh and coo over. No more bright tomorrows with all of our shared joy bubbling over into even brighter tomorrows. All gone.

As I lay immersed in my sorrows, tears streaming down my cheeks, I felt a deep bass vibration in the depths of my soul and it was as if the Lord Himself said to my heart – she has met THE MAN. I caught my breath as I thought of the imagery of Jesus, the Bridegroom and we, the church, as His bride. "Yes, Lord," I whispered. I realized dimly that the reach of my understanding did not extend to eternity and the mysteries beyond. Yet I was also stilled in the turbulence of my grief, comforted that Rebekah's future reality was fully and completely in the hands of God.

I stayed in the warm water, refilling it as needed until I could see through the window that daylight was making its way into the world.

∽ *Rebekah's Journal* ∽

To My Future Husband

I have waited for you these many years
and I am still waiting for you today.
I know that God has you out there for me,
perfectly made for me, the right fit,
but I haven't found you yet.

I pray for you everyday,
but not only you.
I pray for myself.
I pray that I will keep myself pure
and undefiled before God

I also pray that you will do the same thing.
I am saving myself for you
and not just for some guy I decide to "love" one night.
You are the only one I want to share this with.
I want you to know me like no other will.
I have been preparing myself for you.

Not worrying about when I will meet you,
but what kind of woman I will be when I meet you.
will I be a suitable wife?

I just want you to understand
that I will love your faults
even though I am yet to know them.
I am sure of this because I know
that God made you with me in mind.
He knew both of us before we were ever conceived.
our strengths compliment the others' weaknesses,
together we are a whole.

I just want you to know
that I will love everything about you
I may not like you at times,
but I will always love you.

Don't worry;
I know that you are not perfect.
But you are perfect for me.
I keep telling God in our daily chats
that it would be nice if He introduced us,
but He keeps saying not yet.
He knows that I am impatient;
I think that is why he gives me daily lessons in patience.

(continued...)

i hunger to meet you, my love,
for our eyes to finally embrace,
for your voice to wash over me.
will i know you when i see you?
o God, i cannot have gone through my life in vain
only to miss my true love.

open my eyes and heart when he comes along
until then i will wait patiently.

News No One Wants to Hear

I dressed and drove to my office to begin notification of family and others. I called a dear friend, a Vietnam vet, our buddy Bill. When I told him what the police officer had told me, Bill sounded as if he had received a physical punch. His intake of breath was one of pain. "Where are you?" he asked and soon he was at my office, asking how he could help and looking so full of concern. His sweet teenaged daughter, Laura, came in, needing to get to school. Bill assured me that he would be back in touch and I began the phone calls to my family.

My sister Judie lives in Wyoming and when I talked to her she said, "Do you need me to come there?"

I was prepared to be stoic and strong. "No, we'll be alright," I said, "just keep us in your prayers."

"I love you," Judie said.

"I love you, too."

On to the next call, my oldest brother Jerry in Colorado.

I had gotten the speech down pretty well by this time, but the response was still so hard to hear as my brother moaned, "Oh sis."

There are really no words that can possibly speak to the agony of such a loss and nothing that can be said to assuage it. Yet those who love one another look for ways and my big brother wanted so badly to shelter me from such pain.

"What can we do?" he asked.

"Pray for us," I said. "I will need to leave here soon to tell Caleb and Sara. Just keep us in your prayers."

Then the call to my brother Rod, my nearest sibling – both geographically and in age. I caught him at his home in San Francisco.

"Oh, Rona," he replied, as I spoke those words of finality to a precious life.

He too wanted to know what to do. At first I suggested that he call our parents, but then I thought better of it, thinking no, they should hear it from me, and we finished our conversation with his promise to pray for us as well.

I dialed my parent's number, my heart pounding in my throat. Mom answered and I asked if Dad was there. He was not and I was relieved. I told her and she too sounded stricken. Her voice was shaky and she said, "I am so sorry to hear that."

"Me too," I replied. "Me too."

We spoke for a bit more and then I knew that I needed to be on my way for face-to-face meetings with Rebekah's brother and sister.

Sam had arrived at the office and he hugged me as I prepared to go on the darkest journey of my life, to bring news so damaging and sorrowful that I wanted to escape it myself to my two precious children.

∽ *Rebekah's Journal* ∽

"what's it going to be like in eternity with God?"

Frankly, the capacity of our brains cannot handle the wonder and greatness of heaven. It would be like trying to describe the internet to an ant. It's futile...God has given us glimpses of eternity in His word. We know that right now God is preparing an eternal home for us. In heaven we will be...reassigned to do work that we will enjoy doing...we will enjoy unbroken fellowship with God, and he will enjoy us for an unlimited, endless forever."

"why did God really create us?"

I often ask myself this question and I've seemed to keep coming back to the same answer over and over again. God created us because He loves us and wants to have fellowship with us. God does not need us. He doesn't even need us for love or for fellowship, as there is perfect love and fellowship in the trinity. But He created us so that He can spend eternity with us. Maybe that sounds like a simple answer, maybe it is, but that is the answer that I have come to terms with.

The Longest Journey

As I drove to Caleb's apartment I was halfway listening to the Christian radio station that was on in the car. The song said "Looks like the sky above is heavy... feels like the wind is gonna change." Truly the January sky was overcast, gloomy and appropriate. Then the chorus said "Give me the strength to cross this water, Keep my heart upon your altar, Rain Down. Give the strength to cross this water. Keep my feet, don't let me falter." Yes Lord, I thought, give me the strength because I have no idea how I can bear such tidings to Caleb whose tender love for his baby sister was clear to anyone who knew him.

When Caleb had been in the Marine Corps and brought buddies home for the holidays from Camp Pendleton, they would sometimes find out real quick that there were plenty of things that Caleb was carefree and easy going about, but his fierce love and protectiveness about Rebekah became legendary with the uninitiated being briefed on the way to our home. Often young men who came from back east would "camp out" in our living room for the holidays when leave time was not long enough for them to get home.

We could look down on our living room with sleeping bags spread out across the floor and sleepy heads barely showing as we tried to be a replacement family for the fine young Marines over the holidays. Rebekah had an appreciation and affection for all that served in the military, but she had a special devotion for the Marine Corps, because they were her brother's brothers.

As I pulled into the parking area at Caleb's condo, I was praying fervently. My legs felt like rubber as I walked up the sidewalk and knocked on Caleb's door. He opened it to me, dressed in a tee-shirt and sweat pants.

"Hey, Mom," he said with an easy smile.

"Hi, honey. Can I come in?"

He could tell by my voice that something was up and led me in to his home.

"I have some really bad news," I said.

He took my hand.

"Can we sit down?" I asked and he led me to the couch, tenderly holding my hand and smiling a sweet, reassuring smile. "Oh Caleb," I thought, "you have always been able to figure things out, to be three steps ahead in any intellectual challenge, but son, what I will say to you in the next moment is inconceivable and will crush you with its weight". His smile was meant to reassure me, to let me know it was okay, that he would be alright with what I had to say, but I knew his attempt to comfort me in his strength was founded on his ignorance and inability to even envision the vacuum of grief that was about to slam open at his feet.

"Caleb," I said gently, "I have VERY bad news."

He nodded his head, the sweet smile still attempting to reassure. I wondered if the policeman had witnessed that same look on my face, that same confidence that I could hear what he had to say and not be shattered.

"Rebekah was in an auto accident last night," I said and Caleb's face melted, "and she did not survive." It took a moment for the words to register and then Caleb fell to the floor

"Oh dear God," he cried. "Oh dear God!"

I rubbed my hand on his back, silently weeping as his sobs filled the room. Oh, what I would give to shelter him from such pain but I could not and could only be beside him, sharing in his sorrow. He got back up and sat on the couch beside me as his body was wracked with his first wrenching knowledge that his baby sister, his buddy, and his confidante, was passed beyond his ability to hear her laugh, see her smile, share a private inside joke, or just be near.

When he could speak, he looked up at me with red-rimmed eyes and mouthed, "She was my heart!" gently holding his hands over his chest as the sobs renewed.

He leaned over and crumpled on to my shoulder, his tears falling like a sudden downpour as wave upon wave of new realities swept over his soul. For the first time in more than twenty-one years, he would not have two adoring blue eyes watching his every move, longing to hold his hand, hear his voice, and make him laugh. At age twenty-five, Caleb was, for a time, like a child who cries without any reserve, taken completely in their pain. As his sobs became rattled breath and he could cry no more — at least for now — I told him that I still needed to go and tell Sara.

"I will go with you," he stated. "Let me get showered."

While he showered, I wandered into his kitchen, washed some dishes that were in the sink and he laughed when he saw me wiping down counters and cleaning as he came back in to the room.

"I thought I could be doing something," I quipped and he nodded sadly as he slipped on his shoes and socks and we were on our way.

Caleb and Rebekah

⌘ *Rebekah's Journal* ⌘

If I could have one thing in my life right now, it would be to know God's purpose for my life so that I can just set my sights towards that purpose and strive for it. It is so difficult trying to serve God and please God when you feel like you are a fish out of water, frantically flapping around and trying to figure out what in the heck you need to do to get to where God wants you to be!

Sometimes this verse frustrates me: "Thy word is a lamp unto my feet and a light unto my path." It frustrates me because each time I read it, I remember what it means to my life. It means that God will only show me the next step. He will not show me the finish line, but instead leave that in darkness.

So...maybe what it boils down to is what would make me happy is patience. I need to have patience with God (and myself) while working towards my ultimate purpose in life.

Caleb, Sara and Rebekah

Big Sis

We held hands as we drove the ten miles or so to Sara's house. Caleb's presence was a comfort as we pulled up and walked to Sara's door.

It took Sara awhile to answer our knock.

"Hi guys," she said, opening the door.

"Hi, honey," I said with a tired smile.

She looked at Caleb and could tell instantly that something was wrong.

"Can we come in?" I asked and she threw the door open.

I sat down on the couch and put Sara between us. "I have bad news," I said, and Caleb placed his hand on her back, his eyes squeezed closed as if against a blow.

"Sara," I said, holding on to her hand, "Rebekah was in an auto accident last night."

Sara sat staring at me, urging me to go on, "and she did not survive."

"God!" Sara cried, throwing her hands to her face and falling on her knees. "No, not Rebekah."

Caleb and I looked at one another, both of us rubbing her back as she knelt on the floor in front of us. We both knew the desire to reject and throw away such a heinous message. We felt the same – *NO! Not Rebekah!*

As I sat listening to Sara's sobbing I thought that in all of the world could there be a more hated message, a more disgusting fact? Rebekah was a ray of sunshine, a flitting butterfly, she was a lilting note of music, of birdsong and rainbows and joy beaming on the moments of our family life.

In a wounded voice, Caleb whispered, "I will never be an uncle!" He looked at me, disoriented and bewildered by the sadness of that fact. He bent over, swept away in grief again. He and Rebekah had spent many happy hours talking about raising their children together and the joy of introducing them to the same wonders and treasures that they had shared in childhood. Now that all had evaporated before his wounded eyes.

Sara had decided long ago that she would not have children and so Caleb was re-acclimating to a world without Rebekah and the dramatic shift that it brought to his own future landscape as well.

Sara sat back up on the couch, blowing her nose, and catching her breath. "I could see Sam or Ginger," she stated, "but not Rebekah!"

Sam (my husband and Sara's step-dad) had experienced a heart attack a few years earlier and Ginger, our dog, was getting on in years. I understood Sara's line of reasoning. There are things that our mind can conceive because they seem somewhat reasonable, and then there are the inconceivable events that force their way in.

"You had better watch out the next time you come to the house," I quipped. "I'm telling what you said and Ginger will probably bite you!"

Caleb chuckled.

Sara said, "You know what I mean."

"Of course," I said, wrapping my arm around her shoulder.

"I just think of all of the stupid things I have done in my life," Sara said. "If anyone should have gone, it is me.

"It's not a matter of drawing straws," I said. "It was an accident."

"Why Rebekah?" Sara asked. "She was so good. She had so much to offer."

I sat quietly. Sara wasn't expecting an answer. She was shaking with grief and wanting to strike out, fight back.

Time seemed to flutter and move between still frame shots of my two grown children in sadness. We cried and comforted one another and when Sara was finally at the end of her initial sobbing, I prepared to leave. Her fiancé promised that he would look after her.

Sara, Rebekah and Caleb.

Favorite Bible Verse: Proverbs 3: 5-6.

I love this verse because it reminds me that I need to trust in God no matter what. That is often a really hard thing to do because you can think that you know what is best, but God's plan and His timing are different for you.

Also, "Thy word is a lamp unto my feet and a light unto my path." I also like this verse (and hate it) because it reminds me that God will show me what step I need to take, but He will only show me when I need to take that step, not long before.

This is frustrating for me because I like to plan ahead, but I think that due to my impatient nature God wants to teach me patience. So a lot of the time God won't tell me what step that I need to take until I am standing on the screeching edge wondering what in the world I need to do at that moment. I am learning to try and be okay with God not telling me until He is ready.

So frustrating!

Community Tissue Services
A DEPARTMENT OF COMMUNITY BLOOD CENTER

www.cbccts.org

MAIN OFFICE

349 South Main St.
Dayton, Ohio 45402-2715
(937) 222-0228
1-800-684-7783
FAX (937) 461-4225

BRANCHES

708 South Henderson St.
Suite A
Fort Worth, Texas 76104
1-800-905-2556
(817) 882-2556
FAX (817) 882-2557

5425 North First St.
Suite 103
Fresno, California 93726
1-800-201-8477
(559) 224-1168
FAX (559) 229-7217

3450 N. Meridian St.
Indianapolis, Indiana 46208
1-800-984-7783
(317) 916-5254
FAX (317) 916-5255

16361 N.E. Cameron Blvd.
Portland, Oregon 97230
1-800-545-8668
(503) 408-9394
FAX (503) 408-9395

Accredited by
American
Association
of Tissue Banks

January 19, 2004

Rowena Swanson
2420 Bradley
Visalia, CA 93292

Dear Rona and Family,

On Behalf of the entire staff of Community Tissue Services, we extend our deepest sympathy to you and your family during this most difficult time.

It is our sincere hope you will find some measure of comfort in knowing that many people may benefit from your kind and generous decision.

Please accept this medallion in honor of your beloved daughter, Rebekah Swanson.

With our thankfulness and continued support,

Monica Gonzalez, Coordinator
Community Tissue Services – California

Enclosures: Consent, Brochure

Un-niceties

Caleb and I returned to my home and met Sam there. He had closed the office with a message on the door and on the answering machine. "I couldn't stay any longer," he said.

"Of course not," I replied. "Our clients will understand."

Bill called and asked if we had a preference for funeral home. He said he would schedule an appointment for us. We had no idea so he said that he would contact the new Salser and Dillard funeral home because he had heard good things about the owners.

Caleb left to pick up his fiancée Melissa from work and to inform her. She and Rebekah had been friends from junior high.

The phone rang and a young woman identified herself from the organization for organ donors. She expressed her condolences and then said that they had been informed that Rebekah was a designated donor on her driver's license. "It isn't often that we have someone so young who has set up their license that way," she remarked.

"Yes, Rebekah was concerned about others," I said.

"I am calling because I needed to talk with you and walk you through the recorded statement," she said.

"I have not heard back from the coroner's office," I replied.

"Oh," she said. "I am sorry. They have completed their autopsy and that is why I was calling, but I will ask them to contact you."

The coroner's office called a moment later. I went into the guest bathroom and closed the door and asked him to talk to me.

"You are her mother," he said. "I don't want to hurt you."

'I AM her mother," I said. "and I need to know the truth. I have an amazing imagination. I need to be armed with facts in order to keep my mind from tormenting me."

"She died of severe head trauma," he replied. "She had broken vertebrae in her neck due to the impact."

"Did she suffer?" I asked, my voice losing its firmness.

"With the injuries sustained," he said, "she would have died almost instantaneously. The broken vertebrae would cause oxygen to be cut off from the brain."

"Thank you," I said.

"I received a call from the tissue department," he explained. "They will need your recorded permission to have her body released as a donor."

"Okay," I replied, taking a deep breath. "You can have them call me."

The phone rang again and a young woman identified herself as Monica Gonzalez.

"I understand that this is difficult," she said. "but it is important for us to gain your permission for Rebekah to be a donor."

"You are going to be able to use her organs?" I asked.

"No," Monica conceded. "we cannot use her organs since she died at the scene of the accident, but I am calling to ask for tissue donation. With your permission, I will record the release."

"Okay."

"The tape recorder is now on," she said. "My name is Monica Gonzalez and I am calling from the Community Tissue Services, located in Fresno, California. This conversation is being recorded as a legal permit under the Uniform Anatomical Gift Act. Would you please state your name and relationship to the deceased, Rebekah Swanson?"

"My name is Rona Swanson and I am her mother."

"Are you the legal next of kin of Rebekah Swanson?"

"Yes"

"Do you have any objections to the taping of this conversation?"

"No."

"I am asking your permission for the Tissue Bank or applicable agency to remove the following tissues. These tissues may be utilized for transplant if all testing and medical findings are acceptable. Please answer yes or no to the following tissues: Ilia and long bones, (lower legs), including soft tissue, (Ligaments, Tendons, Fascia)"

"Yes."

"Skin."

"Yes"

"Transplant includes life saving, reconstructive and cosmetic surgeries. Multiple institutions, including non-profit and for profit agencies, may be involved in this gift. In addition, while the priority for use of the tissue is in our own area, some portion of the gift may be transported abroad. Do you give permission to all of the above uses?"

"Yes."

"While it is hoped that the gift may be used for transplantation or therapy, it is understood that there is always a possibility that the gift may not be suitable for such use. In that event, the gift can be utilized to advance medical knowledge through medical research, education, and training. Do you give us that permission?"

"Yes."

"Do you grant permission for the testing of blood and tissue for infectious agents including, but not limited to testing of Hepatitis and HIV, to assure medical acceptability of the gift?"

"Yes."

"Do you grant permission for the release of any medical information including hospital records, EMS records, and post-mortem examination reports, to determine suitability?"

"Yes."

"This consent is motivated by humanitarian instincts without the hope or expectation of compensation of any kind. This consent is volunteered without any obligation of any kind on the part of the recipient, hospital, or any individual or organization authorized by law to receive this contribution. Do you have any questions concerning this tissue donation or consent?"

"No."

"Do you grant Community Tissue Services permission to transport Rebekah Swanson to the Community Tissue Services' facility for the purpose of recovery of the tissue donation?"

"Yes."

"Upon completion of the tissue donation the body will be transported to Salser and Dillard Funeral Home. Thank you very much; I am turning off the recorder now."

There was a click as Monica turned off the recording device.

"I want to thank you again for this," she said.

"It is what Rebekah would have wanted, what she did want," I replied. "It is hard for me to give such permission for the use of her body."

"It can save lives. During 9/11, donations like hers helped burn victims survive."

"In life, she was adamant about donating blood as often as she could," I recalled. "It was not as easy for her as it is for me. My veins are simple to find but hers were more bashful and problematic, but she would bite her lip and do it anyway. It meant a lot to her."

"And even now, she is contributing," Monica added.

"Yes," I agreed sadly, "even now."

We rang off and I sat with my head bowed. Even in death, Rebekah was pouring out of herself for others. My mind pictured her body being wheeled into a sterile room and technicians swarming over her, slicing, removing, harvesting. I wanted to scream at the vision. I wanted them to go away, not lay one finger on my child, my precious daughter. I bit my lip and felt the tears flowing once more.

"Lord," I cried. "I just said yes to the salvage crew to go to work on my Beck, against my Mommy's heart but because she would have wanted it that way. Help me to be at peace. Help me to bear this violation of her."

✎ *Rebekah's Journal* ✎

Prayer

God, let me be a willing vessel.
Ready to go where you lead me.
Give me a heart for You
and let me be a servant to Your call.
Give me peace of mind
when You show me Your plans.
Let me be eager to take the first step
even when I don't see the final goal.

News and Photo Albums

The day became a blur after that with Caleb and Missy, his fiancée, coming over. Our friend Bill came by to let us know that he had scheduled appointments for the funeral home, the church, and the cemetery the following day.

He informed us that we should select photos for a slide show for the service and music for the slide show as well.

I was trying to cook something for dinner. I was making spaghetti sauce and the phone was ringing. I left the meat cooking to go into the garage in order to hear whoever was on the other line. It was a reporter from the paper. I wanted to hang up on him but I realized that he was doing his job, and so I prayed to be somewhat lucid as he asked me to describe Rebekah.

"How long have you got?" I joked.

He said, "If you could just tell me a little bit about her."

So I tried, remembering her precocious, adorable baby days to the beautiful accomplished young woman that she had become.

When I came inside, there was Bill, stirring the meat in his suit and tie. I chased him out of the kitchen, calling in to the dining room to Caleb who was pulling out all of our photo albums. When I glanced back in to the living room, Bill had fallen asleep, his head cushioned on the corner of the love seat.

When dinner was ready, I woke Bill up but he said he could not stay.

I mentioned that Sara had called, urging us not to watch the news. Apparently, the accident had been on the news all day. We had not even thought about turning on the TV, but she called to specifically ask us not to.

He nodded his head slowly. "You know what they say in the news business, right?"

"No," I said, shaking my head.

"If it bleeds, it leads." His steel blue eyes held mine. No wonder God had me call this friend to our side. Bill knew about suffering. He knew about loss and he was trying to stand me up for what would not be pretty, to let me know that what I had thought was a very private matter was not private at all.

I nodded back to him.

His face softened. "You're doing just fine," he said, smiling his lopsided smile.

"Don't be too gentle with me," I chided, poking him with my elbow.

"See you tomorrow morning at 10 at the funeral home."

"Tomorrow morning," I replied as he walked out the door.

We spent the evening looking through photo albums, laughing and crying as we selected pictures of Rebekah. I got up from the table to go and look for another album and caught sight of myself in an old antique mirror by the front door. My eyes were swollen so badly that my cheekbones had disappeared, as well as my eye sockets. My eyes were mere slits glimpsed through swollen flesh. I had to laugh and I called back to Caleb, "Why didn't you tell me I looked like this?"

He looked up, smiling a tired smile, and I realized that he looked just the same.

Caleb left with a pouch full of pictures. Missy worked at Kinko's and she was going to blow them up for the slide show and also use some for poster board displays for the funeral home. The plan was for me to meet up with Caleb at 9:30 the next morning to get the copies before all of our appointments.

This Piece of Glass

I look into the mirror
not sure of what it holds for me.
This piece of glass
has become my opponent.
when I look into it
I do not see what others see.
I see a woman who no one would want,
devoid of any beauty.

After a time, I try to listen to people
and see that it may hold something different for everyone.
Terrified of what I might find
I look with much anguish.
I see the person I have become so accustomed to
and wonder how I could have hoped anyone can ever love me.
on second glance, I see a crack in my countenance.
I begin to break it off piece by piece.
Finally, the last piece is removed.
I see someone I don't recognize,
someone with color and life flashing on her face.

who's reflection is this?
I am shocked to find it is me.

Who's to Know?

Night fell and the phone was silent.

Sam and I faced one another, trying to think of tasks that needed to be completed. We tried to think of people that we had not heard from who may not know.

"You need to tell Ken," Sam said.

I shook my head. Later. I would call Ken, my ex-husband, later.

"He is her father," Sam insisted.

"I will tell him," I assured, "just after the service, not now."

"No," Sam said. "You need to tell him now." Sam went and retrieved the recharged phone and handed it to me. "Call him."

So I did, delivering the message of Rebekah's passing calmly and gently as I had learned to do.

Ken was silent and then yelled, "I gotta go." and hung up.

"Well, I told him," I told Sam. "I hope that is the last that we hear of it."

Rebekah, sara, caleb and spike, the cat. .

The Decision

when did I change so much?
I have outgrown
the childish days of my past
and moved on to new horizons,
but I have been forced
to leave all that I know behind.

The people that I know
have not grown with me.
I have remained constant
throughout my life,
growing in my beliefs.
Yet they have changed day by day,
creating new ideals
and new aspirations on a whim.

I cannot keep up with all their changes
and I do not wish to follow their lead.
I strike out on my own road
uncertain of the exact path,
sure of the final destination.

Rebekah's childhood Bible.

Making Arrangements

The next morning Caleb met me in his alley with a packet of photos and Sam and I headed to the funeral home. I had stuffed some CDs into my purse that reflected some of Rebekah's favorite songs. Bill met us in the parking lot and ushered us inside.

One of the directors, Steve Dillard, invited us into his office and we sat down across from him. He led us through some of the preliminaries, where the service would be held, who would speak, selecting the cover and interior of the program for the service and then he asked for photos and any selected music for a slide show.

I pulled out the packet of pictures and put them on the desk.

"Do you have any kind of non-specific music?" Sam asked.

Steve looked at him with a questioning smile, "Non- specific?"

"I was just thinking that surely you have some kind of music that is pretty and pleasant but not tremendously meaningful and profound," Sam explained, "something that I WON'T hear in an elevator or in the produce section of the grocery store. I just thought that it would be better if we put the photos to music that will not overwhelm any of her friends or family afterwards when they are out in public."

"Yes, I understand," Steve said. "We do have instrumental music that we can use that I believe you will find very nice."

"Good," Sam said.

Steve stated that Rebekah's remains had been delivered to the funeral home late the prior evening. He asked how we wanted to handle the viewing. I had not even considered the possibility of having an open casket.

"We could have a viewing?" I asked.

"We can..." Steve said slowly, his soft brown eyes holding my own. "There is swelling. She would not look the same."

"That's okay," Sam said protectively. "We want her to be remembered as she was in life. Anyway, a young woman is concerned about her appearance so we do not want her to be seen at anything less than her best."

Steve looked at me and I nodded. He noted – no embalming – on the form.

"Next, we will need to select a casket," Steve said and rose to lead us to another area. We walked around a casket showroom. The different models and materials were clearly displayed, as well as the prices for each model. I looked at every one of them, feeling a numbing light-headedness as I kept thinking - I am selecting a coffin for Rebekah. It did not take me long to decide. There was a sparkly blue metallic coffin, reasonably priced, that seemed perfect. Even the name – Churchill Blue – seemed a perfect fit. I told Sam my thoughts and he agreed and so we were back in the office again.

Steve mentioned the obituary – what would we want included. I asked for a pad of paper and wrote it out, asking Sam and Bill to read through and approve it.

"I would like to mention a charity in lieu of flowers," I said. "We could name Samaritan's Purse which is Franklin Graham's outreach that was dear to Rebekah's heart. We could name First Assembly or we could name Celebrant Singers."

"Celebrants," Sam said and Bill nodded.

Steve pulled the phone book out for the address and we were finished with the obituary.

We left the funeral home. I had a to-do list of getting back to Steve with the correct spelling of all of the pall bearer's names, once I had contacted and confirmed the men that I wanted to carry her to her final rest.

As we drove away from the funeral home, a sense of panic raced through me like electric shock. I wanted to turn the car around, I wanted to go back, and I wanted to demand to be taken to wherever Rebekah was in that building to touch her, to hold her, to stroke her hand or gently caress her face. It was a physical effort to prevent myself from doing just that, the compulsion was so strong. I knew that her body was there in that building and the longing to be where she rested was almost more than I could bear. I also knew that there was only a small window of time for me to have access to her body, and then it would be buried. The thought of that separation, that loss, pierced like daggers as I drove the short distance from the funeral home to the church.

"Bill," I said. "Can you call Steve and ask him to save some of Rebekah's hair for me?"

Bill looked at me for only a second and then called Steve on his cell phone. "He will make sure he saves a lock of hair for you," he said.

"I know it is only a house that Rebekah has moved out of," I said, trying to explain, "I know she is no longer there. But it is a house that I loved very much. We take pictures of houses where we have lived because of the precious memories."

Bill nodded and I felt so relieved to know I would have a lock of that precious hair.

At the church we met with Pastor Mike Hand. He was in charge of funerals, and we had never really met him before. We talked about who would speak and I asked for Pastor Dennis. He had been Rebekah's youth pastor and just the mention of his name made her face light up. "Yes," said Pastor Mike. "I am sure that Dennis will be happy to speak."

Then he asked about music. I asked if Aaron, the music leader for the college group, The Well, would sing *Heart of Worship* and then Martin and Stephanie (prior Celebrant Singers with Rebekah) would sing *I Can Only Imagine*.

Mike said he would check and find out. He said that Pastor Guerra, our senior pastor, would be there if we wanted him to be and we said, "Please!"

I looked up at Pastor Mike's wall as he was making notes. There was a framed picture with an artist's sketch of a lion and a reference to the scripture regarding the Lion of Judah. I thought how much it reminded me of Aslan, the character of Jesus in the C.S.Lewis books on Narnia. I had to smile because I remembered Rebekah, in sixth grade.

She had taken her Bible to read in her free time. When she had finished her class work, she could read a book of her choosing. She had pulled out her Bible and one of her classmates had acted like she had pulled a rattlesnake out of her backpack.

"You can't have that HERE," her classmate whispered.

"Yes I can," Rebekah replied calmly.

Her classmate shook her head furiously, her eyes wide in terror.

Rebekah stood and walked to the teacher's desk, leaving her friend to cringe in horror.

"Mr. Cates," she said, holding her Bible up in front of him, "I am finished with my homework and wanted to make sure it is okay for me to read this in my free time."

He looked up, smiled and said, "Yes, Rebekah, you may read any book of your choice in your free time."

Rebekah returned to her seat. Her friend thought that Rebekah should be on the same level as Joan of Arc for taking such a courageous stand.

As Rebekah relayed it to me later that day, she found the whole fear over having the Bible in school funny. "God is so remarkable," she said. "People are scared to death to have a Bible in school or to mention God...yet *The Lion, the Witch, and the Wardrobe* is required reading! There is Jesus, as clear as day in Aslan, and yet, no one sees Him."

———————

There in Pastor Mike's office, looking up into the face of Aslan, the Lion of Judah (and Narnia) I was comforted with the knowledge that Rebekah knew exactly who He was and is as we planned her service.

We saw Dennis – Rebekah and Caleb's youth pastor – on our way out and he gave me a big hug. He said he would be honored to speak, and I asked him if he would serve as a pallbearer as well. "Yes," he said and then he asked about Caleb.

"Keep him in your prayers," I said. "He has lost a big chunk of his heart!"

Dennis nodded and we were on our way again, out to the cemetery.

∞ *Rebekah's Journal* ∞

Searching

A fire burns deep within
its embers ever glow.
The word of God fans its flames
and makes my spirit burn for Him.
I hunger to know His will.
I long to know
His plans for me,
searching every day
to find the next step I must take.
Bringing me closer to my final goal.

11

Plotting Together

We stood at the counter waiting for one of the women to come and assist us.

When she approached, our buddy Bill, who had scheduled each of the appointments at funeral home, church, and cemetery said, "This is for Rebekah Swanson."

The woman talked about grave sites and interment fees, and she talked about double plots and singles. We had never purchased a cemetery plot. This was new ground that we were covering but it seemed to make sense that we would snatch up the neighboring properties so that we could all "rest in peace" together. A helper took us out in a cart to look at available sites.

"I was born here in Visalia and I will be buried here," Bill said as we looked across the green grass dotted with gravestones and flowers.

As we drove to one area, we went past a section of the cemetery that was very familiar to me. Every year on Memorial Day, we attended the service. As the years went by, Rebekah, Caleb, and I were seated together. Then it was Rebekah and I as her brother played in the band. Then came a time when I sat alone and Rebekah and Caleb were in the band together. I remembered the one year when Caleb, fresh from Marine Corps Boot Camp, came in his dress blues while Rebekah played in her high school band uniform, so proud of her big brother. Then he was off to serve in the Corps and Rebekah and I were attending without him.

Now we found ourselves at a piece of lawn not far from all of those fond memories, a place that had heard every note of the music played over the years and that would enfold Rebekah in her final rest. I stood looking back towards the spot where the band played and said, "This will be fine."

We talked about the fact that we could give Rebekah the bottom bunk and I could take the top...then Sam could be across the aisle. It seemed only appropriate that our precious maiden daughter and I could bunk together, I thought, my mind wandering to the many times that we had bunked together at family reunions and on trips.

"Hey, Bill," Sam asked, bringing me out of my reverie, "do you have your place picked out?"

"Not yet," Bill replied.

"I got a bunk to sublet," Sam said. "If you want bottom bunk, I already know what I will have put on the headstone," Sam continued, holding his hands up to help us envision the marquee message. "It'll say, 'Bill, quit grabbing my ass!'"

Bill and I cracked up standing out there in the bare grass. It felt good to laugh, even as we selected burial plots. There was also something comforting in watching my dear husband, whose greatest weapon is his humor, and our dear friend find some laughter in the somber duties we were performing together.

We rode back and purchased three plots so that Sam and I could be buried there as well, with the promise that the sublet offer was open should Bill want to be a neighbor.

We stood out in the cemetery parking lot as Bill consulted his legal pad.

"Funeral home, church, and now the cemetery," Bill said, checking off his list. "You still need to call Steve at the funeral home with the pallbearer's names for the program."

"I will," I promised, making a note to myself.

"Then I think that's it for now," Bill said. "Why don't you guys go on home, and I'll check in with you later."

We both gave Bill a big hug and Sam and I headed home.

Reminders

I think of you
when the wind blows
through the trees.
That is how I view you
something I can
neither touch nor see.

I think of you
when the tides turn,
moving up the beach.
That is how I feel you,
ever moving and changing,
something I can never keep.

I think of you
when the sun sets
and leaves my world dark.
That is how I live
every day when you leave
the orbit of my life.

I think of you
when the flowers bloom
and die each the year.
That is how I am with you

(continued...)

blooming in your presence,
vibrant and dying when you leave.

I think of you
when I cry my salty tears
feeling so alone.
That is what happens
when you are not near to me,
nothing makes sense now.

Sweet Voices

The answering machine was beeping like mad when we got home and we began taking down names and numbers as sweet voices came on with messages of love and support. One dear voice said, "Look out your front door. We left you some things and call if we can help!" Outside the door were grocery bags full of salads and fruit and coffee and coffee cakes and fresh flowers and so many other loving items that Cecilia and Tracy, our dynamic duo, had gone out and purchased for us. "We know you won't feel like cooking but you might want something to nibble on or something if people come by, so it's just a little thing that we could do. WE LOVE YOU!" the message said. Cecilia had lost her mother after a long battle with cancer. She knew the numb sleep-walk that we were in and she wanted to help.

Mrs. Curtis, Rebekah's third grade teacher, came by, her face swollen and red from crying. She clutched a potted hydrangea and had a card signed by all of the teachers at Mineral King Elementary School where Rebekah and Caleb had attended and where I still volunteered. She could barely speak but whispered, "We are praying for you," as she passed the lovely plant to me.

The rest of the day faded into night as call after call came in. I would have to end one call to take a new call only to take another new call. Our portable phone ran out of juice and I was left with the old stationary phone upstairs in our bedroom. Somewhere in the midst of all of the calls and all of the voices the news came that my brothers and their wives and my sister were coming! What a tremendous blessing. My older siblings were on the way! Judie would stay at our home while the big brothers were arranging for hotel stays.

Unknown Comfort

Let me take you in my arms
And calm your tired spirit
While I hold you in my hands

Let me soothe your saddened heart
Allow me to break off each piece of pain
-one by one-
tenderly from your soul
I will bury them each
In the depths of the ocean
Never to be found

And there in the peace
We will hold each other
And God's spirit will pour over us
And heal our broken hearts.

E-notification and Reluctant Cleansing

I realized that I should send out an e-mail to some of the families that we corresponded with regularly. Sam had brought my laptop computer home, and I put together an e-mail to them to let them know what had happened.

I went into the bathroom that Judie would be using to tidy it up. It had been Rebekah's bathroom when she was home from school and I had not cleaned it since she had moved back to her college dorm just days before. As I scrubbed the bathtub and then moved to the sink, my mind was racing over the impossible fact that only 4 days before Rebekah had been here. I was about to sprinkle cleanser in the sink when I looked down and saw a small glob of toothpaste left in the sink, the kind of little glob left when you spit and do not rinse the sink well. I froze in place. I could not sprinkle cleanser on Rebekah's spit glob. She would never spit in that sink again. How could I possibly remove her final toothpaste spit so callously?

Sam came and stood in the doorway. He could see my gaze riveted on the glob of dried toothpaste.

"Hey, honey," he said, waiting for me to look up at him "If I die while I'm on the toilet, for God's sake – *FLUSH!*"

That was it. I shook the canister and cleaned the sink in anticipation of my sister's arrival the next day.

Sam and Rona's wedding...
with Sara, Rebekah and
Caleb in the wedding party.

Rainbows In Your Eyes

Your tears flowed down freely today.
Flooding me in a wave of sadness.
I felt your grief upon my heart,
submerging me in your pain.
I wanted to wipe away every tear
and see the rainbows in your eyes once again.
For when the pain is gone
you will be even more beautiful than before.

The trials of the years
have only made you stronger.
I can see the strength in your eyes
behind your broken down heart.
You are a pillar of strength
among the turmoil of this chaotic world.
For tomorrow, your eyes will once again shine
with rainbows brought on only by tears.

Demands

Caleb called. "Mom, Dad says that we need to get Rebekah's name right on the announcement."

"It is right," I said.

"He keeps saying it better say his name," Caleb said through gritted teeth.

"I'll talk to him," I promised.

"You shouldn't have told him," Caleb said.

"Sam wanted me to be sure and notify him, you know, out of courtesy," I explained.

Sam had come to stand beside me and he told Caleb, "I will take care of it, son."

"Okay," Caleb said.

It had been over 18 years since we had lived with Ken. It took a restraining order and staying for a month with the Sheriff and his wife in order to get away from his abusive behavior. When the judge granted me the privilege to go back to my maiden name, I was delighted as I proudly displayed my new driver's license. The children asked me to take them along, hungry to snip the ties to the ugliness and cruelty that they had tasted from their dad and his family. We lived in a small town and the teachers changed the last names of the children on report cards, etc. Since Rebekah was the youngest, she never had a report card, immunization record, student achievement award, or any other document that did not say Rebekah Marie Swanson. Only her birth certificate stated otherwise. As she went through her life her driver's license, Social Security Card and her beloved passport all stated Swanson.

Sam dialed Ken's number.

"Hello, Ken? This is Sam... Oh, I'm doing okay. But I am calling because Caleb said you are demanding things you shouldn't be. Ken, Rebekah never introduced herself as anything other than Swanson her entire life. The announcements will read Swanson, nothing more... *capice?*"

There was a long pause and then Sam said, "Good night."

I was so proud of Sam. He was firm, concise and calm, and he handled Ken.

Trade

Draw this breath from me
and fill yourself up too.
Take a portion of my life
and mold it into yours.
Give yourself the joyful glow
of those who love you.
Keep a piece of my heart
and lend me part of yours.

Precious in the Sight of the Lord

My eyes open in the night. I keep waking up at 2:30 AM, well before dawn. I came fully awake with a quick intake of breath. Then the thought – Rebekah is not here. I went to check e-mail and read in the darkness an e-mail from our friend Pastor Marc Unger.

––––––––––

Subj: Standing with you in prayer
Date: 1/16/04 12:16:11AM Pacific Standard Time

Dear Sam and Rona,
I just read your e-mail. I am STUNNED! There are no words. Lynda and I grieve with you in holy silence and intend to support you this Saturday. I copied your e-mail into Daniel's letter tonight. Brother and sister, our hearts go out to you and your family in deepest sympathy, prayer and in the love of our Lord and Savior Jesus Christ.

Psalm 116:15 Precious in the sight of the Lord is the death of His godly ones.
Psalm 116:16 O Lord, surely I am Thy servant , the son of Thy hand-maid, Thou hast loosed my bonds.
Psalm 56:8 Thou hast taken account of my wanderings; Put my tears in Thy bottle; Are they not in thy book?

We tearfully stand with you in this unspeakable tragedy.
All our love in Jesus Christ,
Pastor Marc, Lynda, Daniel, David, Elizabeth, and Anna

––––––––––

I sat on my knees in Rebekah's room. The only light was the gentle glow of the computer screen. I stared at the screen, unable to take in the statement that somehow Rebekah's death could be called precious.

Lord, my heart cried, how could her death be precious to You? I will not move from this place, I cannot move from this place until you help me understand that somehow you can call what to me is utter destruction and ruin a precious thing.

Tears streamed down my cheeks as I read and re-read...Precious in the sight of the Lord...Precious in the sight of the Lord.

As I thought back over the sweetness of our relationship my heart ached. I felt as if I stood on a precipice, gazing into nothingness. Echoes of her voice and laughter and love were enshrouded in the cloudy darkness that fell away at my feet.

Precious in the sight of the Lord...*precious?* Lord, I do not know how this can be precious to you, so I will just trust you and I will hold it as precious. I will hold this tenderly and gently, and I will go slowly. Light my path and hold my hand for I feel so undone.

⤳ *Rebekah's Journal* ⤳

I think that when we are at different points in our lives, things stick out to us a lot more than they would at other more normal times in our existence. we see things differently. we even seem to breathe the air in differently, like we are doing it for the first time and experiencing it's lushness all anew. The books we read, the movies we watch, the verses we like all change with our mood, with our place in life, with our relationship with God. I don't always like change that much, but I guess that I better love it because when you stop changing you're dead.

change is beautiful.

Shiva

Friday morning. Nowhere to go but I hit the shower early. My mind was spinning with all of the things that I needed to be sure were done and ready as guests would begin arriving.

As the water poured down on me, my tears let loose as well.

And I remembered Tuesday night, while Rebekah still lived. I had arrived home later than usual. Sam was upstairs playing his trumpet. I was alone downstairs in the kitchen cooking dinner. From across the room and from a cabinet that was closed, I saw a glass vase fall from the top shelf. It landed on the edge of the tile counter, breaking in two and then fell to the floor where it shattered, no, it disintegrated, into a million pieces. I had been startled when I saw the movement and could do nothing but watch as it broke once and then descended to the floor with devastating effect. The force of the smashing had sent shards into the living room and dining room. It had taken me a long time to sweep and clean and wipe and clean some more until I could be sure that the pieces were all gathered up.

I did not know why I would be recalling that strange occurrence and then, suddenly, I felt God whisper to my shattered heart. "I knew before the accident happened. With that vase, I let you see what would happen before it ever occurred. I know where every broken shard lies."

I stood motionless as the water beat down.

God knew. He knew. BEFORE!

I could see that falling vase, whole and complete, then breaking in two, then the impact and the sharp, glassy missiles flying everywhere like dangerous confetti.

"God," I whispered slowly. "I know you are loving. I know you are strong. I don't know why you did not prevent it, but you do not have to answer to me! I just know that if you don't put me back together, all is lost. Please, please, if you know where all of the pieces flew, please mend my shattered heart."

My sister would be in later that day. My brothers and their wives would be arriving as well. A cousin and her family were on their way. The only house guest would be my sister but I tried to pull myself together and vacuum and dust and straighten the house a bit. The doorbell rang and there stood a deliveryman with a beautiful orchid and right there behind him was a dear friend and long-time client, Lauralee.

"I just came here to give you this," she said, enfolding me in her arms. Her smile was as sweet as always. I had stopped by their business on that fated evening on my way home from my own office with some paperwork for her. In fact, her daughter was planning to contact Rebekah to glean some college application pointers. I had bragged about Rebekah.

The prior weekend Rebekah had told me, "Mom, you know how I like to plan things?"

I nodded.

"I just can't see the future," she said with a frown, "I don't know what's next."

I had laughed and had put on my most dramatic movie announcer voice as I pointed my fingers toward the make-believe marquee. "Adventure, Romance, Excitement," I enthused. "THAT is what your future holds!"

I had shared that story with Lauralee at her office the evening that Rebekah died. I could tell Lauralee was remembering too and her sweet eyes were such pools of compassion and concern. "You doing okay?" she asked.

I nodded. "As well as we can," I admitted and she understood.

The doorbell rang and the people identified themselves as representatives of Fresno Pacific, Rebekah's university.

Lauralee hugged me again and was gone.

The dear people from Rebekah's school wanted to help, to comfort, to serve. I am sure that in many households the presence of others is desired. However, this was the first time that I was meeting these folks and so it felt like a burden to entertain or converse. Even as I was feeling burdened, I was also feeling guilty about feeling burdened. I realized, or maybe the Holy Spirit instructed me with a bit of a pinch, that it takes a very courageous soul to come to a home where such a loss has occurred. I realized that this visit was a gift, it was what they knew to do, and so I just let them sit with me and fulfill the commandment to comfort one another.

I was continually answering the phone because Sam had gone to the office to check on mail and messages.

After a time, they prepared to take their leave and once again expressed their sympathy and promised to keep us in their prayers.

"Thank you," I replied. "I can sincerely say that I feel those prayers. They are what is holding us all together."

⤳ *Rebekah's Journal* ⤳

When my uncle was younger, he wrote on his ceiling in glow in the dark paint "what did you do today?" so that every night before he went to sleep he would ponder that. At the end of the day, if you pondered that question what would bring you joy to know that you had accomplished it?

I would want to be able to say that I lived life to the fullest, that I loved people without holding back and being afraid of how I will be hurt by being vulnerable to them.

It's not about a certain act that you did, but making sure that you vibrated with God's love. I'd also like to be able to think "I went to the Parthenon today or I swam in the Great Barrier Reef." But without my own selfish desires it would just be that I loved people the best I could and with the love that God wants me to have for them and made that known to them.

What did you do today?

Prayer

I'm praying for you
I know that's not what you want to hear
But that's what I have to say

I'm praying for you
Because I love you
And this is the best gift that I can give.
You ask me how I can love you
with such fullness, no holding back

I love you because God first loved me!
Everything I have,
Everything I can give
Comes from Him, not from me.

I love you because He gave me all of the love
which I hold inside of me
He's given me every ounce that I now freely give to you.
Today and everyday, I will pray for you.
That through me, you will know and feel
God's love for you!

A Weary Stand

Silence but not for long. The phone rang and it was Sara.

"Mom," she moaned. "Dad is saying he is going to sit with us tomorrow. He says he wants to be between Caleb and me."

I heaved a heavy sigh and told her I would talk to him.

I had not been off the phone for a minute before Caleb called, explaining that Ken had been calling him, telling him how things would be at Rebekah's service the next day. Unlike Sara, who was sad, Caleb was angry at the intrusion and furious over the shameless insinuation of himself into our private grief.

I knew that I would have to call Ken. I would have to address him and try to make him understand why it would not be possible for him to be welcomed into the warm and loving embrace of our grieving hearts. That I would have to explain it once again was proof of the tragic nature of his blind selfishness.

I called Ken and asked if he had been calling Caleb and Sara.

"Yes," he said. "I want to be sure that I will be able to sit with them tomorrow."

"They do not want to sit with you, Ken," I replied.

"I am their father."

"You are."

"I need to be there with them," he said.

"You will only cause them more pain with your presence," I stated.

"You think I don't have pain?"

"I am sure that you do," I replied. "I cannot alleviate that."

I remembered Christmas Day 2003, only a few days before Rebekah's death. Sam and Rebekah and I were unwinding after all of the guests had gone home. The phone rang and Beck had answered it, her voice chirping out, "Hello!" but then her expression had changed. The lilt in her voice became a monotone, dead and lifeless. She came and sat at my feet and had a monosyllabic response for whatever was being said on the other end of the line each time she spoke. I knew who had called and I knew why her joy had turned to guarded dread. When the call was over, she said that she wished that she did not have to speak to her father on holidays, and it led to a long talk that evening about her relationship to him. He had wounded her deeply, emotionally as well as physically, when she was a child.

"I have forgiven him, Mom," she said. "I had to, for my own sake. The kind of rage and hurt I felt for him was a toxin that would poison my relationships with other men. I have forgiven him...but I have no idea how to relate to him, how to have any contact with him. He will not acknowledge any wrong. He tries to make me feel like I am a nut if I talk about his abuse. Instead, he wants to talk about how I have failed him as a daughter. I don't call, I don't write, I don't come and see him. What he does not understand, what he refuses to comprehend, is that even the sound of his voice, the mention of his name is a wound to me."

"I hated hearing your voice on the phone tonight," I admitted. "You sounded dead. I do not know what I would do if you ever spoke to me that way."

"I can't help it," Rebekah replied. "That was my best attempt to be civil. My best attempt to override my disgust. Maybe someday I will manage it," she said with a shrug of her shoulders.

"I think you have done all you can, sweetheart," I said, wrapping her in my arms. "You can't make someone else change or repent. You can only release their hold on you by letting go of the hate."

"I have and I will continue to do it when it rises up," she said, "but let's make a deal."

"Okay?"

"Let's not answer the phone on holidays any more!" she suggested with a weary smile.

"I have a compromise proposal," I countered. "Let's make sure we know who is calling before we agree to talk, agreed?"

"Agreed!"

Now here I was, at the other end of the phone line with the grief giver again.

"Ken," I said. "You need to know that Rebekah forgave you. We talked about it a lot recently. As a young woman, she needed to be set free from the hurt and anger that she carried around. She had chosen to forgive you but she had no clue how to relate to you, how to talk with you, how to have any semblance of a normal relationship with you."

"Why?"

"Why?" I laughed. "You cannot be serious. Truly."

"I never did anything to her to hurt her."

"Oh, I will not bear this now. My heart is broken. I am in pieces over losing Rebekah but I will not stand for your lies. Not now. Not ever again. You hurt her for your own sick reasons. She bore the scars. And to multiply your sin, you told her that if she spoke of it, you would hurt Caleb and Sara. You can deny it, you can tell yourself it never happened, but it did."

"I don't know what you are talking about."

"But I do. You wounded a child. She was too small, too innocent, and too afraid to understand. But when she got older, when she could understand, when she could begin to unravel the fear and the pain and the hurt, that was when she was able to tell me about it and cry and grieve and forgive."

"I never hurt her."

"That is a lie."

"If I did, I don't remember."

"Ask God to help you."

Silence.

"As to tomorrow, I want to ask you not to come to the service. Caleb and Sara are bearing enough right now."

"Are you saying that I shouldn't attend the funeral?"

"That's right."

"You're saying that I am not welcome at my own daughter's funeral?"

"That is EXACTLY what I am saying. The only people who would know if you attend or not are the very ones asking you to stay away."

"I can't believe it."

"Please believe it," I said. "I could not be any more clear if I had hit you in the face with a cast iron skillet to get your attention. You are not wanted. Your presence will only add to the weight your children are bearing. You have an opportunity, for just once in your role as a father, to put your children before yourself. You have this glorious opportunity opening before you. You can tell them that you will not come. That you will honor their wishes. That you realize that now is not the time to try and add anything to the difficulty of the public service for their baby sis."

"They didn't call and tell me this!"

"No," I agreed, "they called me. They do not know how to make you listen. I think that has always been the problem. You don't have ears to hear what they are saying. So let me be clear. We will know by your actions how you feel about your children. If you set aside your wishes and honor theirs, you may lay the first plank in a bridge to a future with them. It is too late for that with Rebekah, but you have two grown children who are still alive and who really would like to have a relationship with you based on mutual respect. They are adults. They are really great people. It is a shame that you do not know them, and maybe you can start with this first step."

"I will have to talk it over with Mary."

"What?" I replied. "Don't be silly. Mary would not insist that you attend if you explain the situation."

"I have to discuss it with my wife."

"Fine. Just let me know what you decide."

Silence.

"Will you do that?"

"I will talk it over with Mary."

"Your decision will be clear — either you respect Caleb and Sara or you don't."

"Goodbye."

"Goodbye."

I dialed the church and asked for Pastor Mike. I hated to do it but thought he should be aware of the controversy.

"Oh, yeah," he said. "He has been calling me a bunch. He wanted me to change the obituary. He wanted me to change the service. All kinds of demands. I have explained to him that I don't know him and he is not the one calling the shots."

"How did he handle that?"

"He got all friendly and accommodating," laughed Mike. "I told him that we will have a video tape of the service. I offered to send it to him."

"And..."

"He said he had to be there, as the father."

"Oh, Mike, I asked him – no practically begged him – not to come."

"Maybe he won't," Mike offered.

"Wouldn't that be nice?" I said.

Becoming one

Drip drip
The tiny drops of water form
so quietly on the branch
Holding a secret in their depths

Drip
It falls so quickly
into the lake
Building to a breaking point
where it can no longer hold on

Drip
It drops to its death
Becoming one with an immortal being
changing from being a lonely drop
To a small part of a big lake

Drip
such a meaningless being
somehow begins to matter
when you realize this big lake
Is made up of millions of drops of dew
Drip, drip

Crowded Home

My sister Judie arrived and then a stream of people began to flow through the house. Out of town guests and Rebekah's college friends swelled the living room. Jackie, her roommate, had brought a frame with pictures of Rebekah beautifully matted in it. I put it right at the top of a cabinet in our living room. I could look at it every day. I had such an underlying sense of needing to chase after Rebekah that having her smiling face right there was a comfort.

In the midst of the hubbub, Pastor Mike called to say that Ken had been in touch and they were not going to attend the service the next day. It was a relief that I shared with Sara and Caleb. The news was a visible lift to their spirits.

Rebekah's friends made a circle on the floor around me in the living room. They had gone to the funeral home viewing. They said it was beautiful with music and video and flowers and big posters of Rebekah's pictures. The casket was closed so there was really no "viewing" in that respect, but they said that people had been coming by and that the pictures brought lots of smiles.

Just seeing their sweet faces was a comfort to me. Those familiar faces and voices eased my aching heart. We talked and laughed. Someone was serving food and drinks and there were crowds of people all throughout the downstairs.

At one point I leaned back against the wall, closed my eyes and just listened to the stories and laughter and general noise of all of the sweet people gathered around. While my heart was crying out in loss over Rebekah, it was also soothed by those who loved her so.

The guests went home and we got ready for bed. I had no trouble falling asleep at night but I came suddenly and completely awake in the dark. Every time the clock turned to 2:30am I was awakened with a gasp and then the realization – Rebekah is gone.

Maybe it's just me and the need to have something tangible to believe in, but I would love to talk to Jesus. I think it would be so awesome to hear the parables from him and to realize that you are in the presence of the son of God.

I'd love to meet my grandmother. The stories everyone tells about her are so intense. My grandmother died of cancer when my mom was a little girl. My mom would go and visit her every day after school at the hospital and my grandmother never spoke of pain. But she was dying and in horrible turmoil. She had bruises on her hips from all the shots and must have been suffering a lot, but she acted like everything was normal for my mother's benefit. She was such a strong woman.

I often wonder how my mom's life (and thus mine) would have been different if my grandmother had lived. My mom had 2 stepmothers after that (her first stepmother died of cancer, too). But that's who I would like to meet. Such a strong woman and role model.

From Paralytic to
Carrying My Own Stretcher

I got up quietly and went downstairs to the kitchen. I put a pot of coffee on to brew. As I waited for the fragrant pick-me-up, I began thinking about the service that we would be expected to attend in about seven hours. I felt so very weak that I wondered if I would even be able to walk in to the church building from the car under my own steam. I wondered if they would have to carry me in like the man whose friends lowered him through the ceiling for Jesus to heal. My legs felt like overcooked spaghetti and just the thought of having to face people in a public setting when I was hurting so deeply made me cringe.

The coffee finished and I poured myself a mug. I went into the darkened living room and put on a worship CD, the volume turned very low. I sat on the love seat Indian style with both hands wrapped around the warmth of the mug, my face bent over the fragrant steam rising. I breathed it in and could not remember when I had eaten last. I had not been hungry and had not thought of food, except to offer it to others. As I sat in the darkness, the music changed to a deep throbbing bass drum beat. Then the lyrics began. "How lovely is your dwelling place, O Lord Almighty. For my soul longs and even faints for You, For here my heart is satisfied within your presence, I sing beneath the shadow of Your wings."

I felt the tender protective presence of God enfold me as I listened to those sweet words. The song was very familiar, one that I had sung often with Rebekah. Then the chorus began and my heart melted away as I joined in surrender. "Better is one day on your courts, better is one day in your house, better is one day in your courts, than thousands elsewhere."

I thought of the tender reality of Rebekah's being. She was now in the presence of a Holy, Loving God. Better, yes better, than the thousands of days that I felt cheated out of. Better, Lord. Better is one day than thousands elsewhere. Help me to survive the holocaust of the thousands here that I long for. Help me to see it from eternity's angle and to know that it is better for her. I will never again see her cry a tear of pain, never again ache when her heart is broken, never again, for she is safely in your House. "My heart and flesh cry out for you the Living God, your Spirit's water to my soul. I've tasted and I've seen. Come once again to me. I will draw near to you. I will draw near to you!"

I sang along with the CD. Tears were flowing down my cheeks as I proclaimed with the singers, "Better is one day in your courts, better is one day in your house, than thousands elsewhere. "Yes, Lord," I prayed. "I surrender my precious Rebekah to you. She was yours before I ever knew her. You loved her first and you have kept her soul safe and secure."

I continued to listen to the music as I drank my coffee. I got up for a refill and let the worship music wash over me, soothing and warming me with the adoration of God.When the music finished I took out the slide show video that the funeral home had put together for the service. They had sent a copy to us and I slid it into the player. The pictures were lovely and I wept as I looked at the different scenes of Rebekah as a baby, gazing at her big brother, sitting among wildflowers with Caleb and Sara. Riding horses and growing up, dearer and more lovely with each passing year. When the 20 minute video came to an end, I re-wound it and watched it again. I was able to view the scenes without weeping the second time and I re-wound it once again and the third time through I was rejoicing over a remarkable life, so well-lived, so full of love and laughter and grace and beauty.

I got up and began making some boiled eggs for breakfast. I thought it would probably be good to eat something. I knew that I would need some fuel for what lay ahead.

I made some toast and sliced some fruit for Sam and Judie to have when they woke up.

It was now day and I had consumed plenty of caffeine. I put a fresh pot of coffee on just as Judie made her way downstairs.

"How are you doing?" she asked.

"Much better," I said. "When I first got up I did not think I would be capable of even crawling in to the service but I feel able to face it now."

We all got showered and dressed and made our way to the hotel where family was staying. The funeral home sent a limousine for us there and we all went to the church.

They took us in a side door and there were my brothers and their wives and Judie and my cousin and her husband and daughter. Our pastor came and prayed with us. I told him that God had given me such peace, even in the midst of such loss. He nodded his head as he looked at me. His face was stiff as he looked around at all of us. How dear to see my brothers and their sweet wives. What a comfort to have them there. Just looking at their precious faces was soothing to my wounded heart. Their sweet smiles spoke peace and healing. I understood much more fully the meaning of Jacob in the Bible when he told Esau that when he saw his face it was like seeing the face of God. I felt the same, gazing at those beloved faces!

∽ *Rebekah's Journal* ∽

I have every goal of touching lives and reaching people for Christ. Part of me wants to throw away all the conventions and all the ideas of what a "proper job" is and maybe even all the education I have earned and become a missionary. There is something about living in a state where you have to trust God for survival and living every day just to be able to speak to people about God's love. Maybe it's a passing phase, but at the same time it's kept coming back since my senior year of high school and I keep pushing it away because it isn't the worldview of success. It's a sacrifice.

Hmmm...maybe I shouldn't have talked about that, but that's my mind jabbering on. I love being able to show people how very much they mean to God.

A Celebration of Life

Soon we were ushered into the sanctuary and there was a huge portrait of Rebekah in front of us. Sam moaned as we were walking and I whispered, "Just keep breathing, just keep breathing," imitating Dory from *Finding Nemo*. Sara was right in front of Sam and she snickered and smiled back at me. Nemo was her favorite movie, so it let her think of something sweet in the middle of a very difficult walk.

Once seated our pastor came out and welcomed everyone to the service. "Today is a sad day, but we want to think of it as a celebration of a life well lived."

And so it began. There was a framed photo of Rebekah directly in front of us, and I found myself looking into her eyes throughout the service, smiling at her as people said wonderful things about her.

Our friend Bill read the obituary:

REBEKAH MARIE SWANSON
November 19, 1982 – January 13, 2004

Rebekah Marie Swanson passed away Tuesday, January 13, 2004. She was a student.

Rebekah was born in Bakersfield but spent her first five years in the Sierra foothills in Glennville. Apricot hair and cornflower blue eyes, she was precocious and charming. As she grew and her family moved to Visalia, she attended grade school at Mineral King Elementary to Valley Oak Junior High and then Golden West High School. She was an eager student, an enthusiastic adventurer, and blessed many lives with her warm and loving presence.Rebekah was to graduate from Fresno Pacific University this spring with a double major in English and Psychology.

Instead, she has graduated early to her heavenly home. Her love of God and her desire to share the love of Christ was her driving passion.

She is survived by her mother, Rona Swanson; her step-father, Sam Tomaino; her brother Caleb Swanson and his fiancé Melissa

Kirksey; her sister Sara Swanson; her grandparents Ray and Donna Swanson and loving aunts, uncles, cousins and countless friends.

Aaron Albright sang one of Rebekah's favorite songs *Heart of Worship*. It was sweet to hear it and think about the times when we sang it together to the Lord.

Then Dennis, her youth pastor, spoke. He admitted that he had questioned *WHY?* when he heard of Rebekah's accident. He talked about her smile and her focus on making sure she put the things of God in the first place in her life. How lovely to know that she lived her life in a way to not be ashamed when her finish line occurred.

The final song was *I Can Only Imagine*, sung by Martin and Stephanie. "Surrounded by your glory, what will my heart feel, will I dance for you Jesus, or in awe of you be still, will I stand in your presence or to my knees will I fall, will I sing Hallelujah, will I be able to speak at all? I can only imagine."

For those of us in the service, it was a sweet reminder that one day, one day we will no longer just have to imagine what being swallowed up in light and love is like.

After the service, a side room was set up with food and tables for a reception. Sam, Caleb, Sara and I stood over along the wall for people to come and speak to us if they wished. It became a long line snaking through the room and out the doors. It reminded me of a wedding but of course it was not. So many sweet faces, teachers and classmates, the crew from Borders books where Beck had worked, people that I had never met but who wanted to tell us what Rebekah had meant to them.

When the line cleared and we were able to take seats at one of the tables, Bill played a song that my oldest brother's daughters had recorded for us. The room grew silent and then those sweet voices of Rebekah's beloved cousins – Serena and Wendy – filled the room.

Rebekah's Song

To give a smile when you are down,
    To be a friend when no one is around
A helping hand when you're in need
    A caring heart, someone who sees
This is my prayer
This is my song
That with Jesus you'd come along

That you would know the Savior's love
And that you too would live up above.
So say goodbye and cry a tear,
   But please remember the Father is near
We'll meet again on that shore
   Where this old world won't matter any more

Sam and I smiled at one another as we listened to the sweetness of their voices and their tribute to their younger cousin.

Then Bill passed the microphone and friends and professors and family shared intimate memories of our Rebekah. It was so good to be surrounded by those who loved her so very much. We were all so very aware of what we had lost, even as we struggled to come to grips with that reality.

Finally, we left, with Bill promising to follow with all of the food that the women had prepared for us.

When we got home, there were stacks and stacks of cards and letters that had been left at the service and at the funeral home. I spent the afternoon reading and weeping over the sweet messages of love and caring.

There was a folder full of letters from the crew at Borders book store where Rebekah had briefly worked. Her plan was that she would be able to transfer to England where she planned to pursue her Master's degree. She said it would enhance her application if she could show that she would have a position there once in England.

One was prefaced "For those who loved Rebekah: She was the sweetest human I have ever met and even though I only knew her three months, I will remember her always."

"I had only known Rebekah for two months, but from my first day at work, her smile lit me up for the day. I would always look for her when I got there and when I left. She was a great person."

"Rebekah was one of the kindest and most lovable people I've ever met in my life. She was beautiful and everyone knew it. I don't think I ever remember a time when Rebekah didn't stay after shift to talk to us. I never at any time heard anything come out of her mouth but the most genuine and loving thoughts."

"I only knew Rebekah for a short time, but I dearly loved her. She was a sweet and kind person. She made me want to be a better person, just by being herself."

"She was everyone's friend and it was not difficult to fall in love with her. I will miss her!"

"I knew Rebekah for only three short months. For half of that time I worked at the registers where she also worked. During the time spent as cashier I got to know Rebekah through casual conversations and meaningful conversation. She always greeted me so kindly and with a smile- something so simple that some people don't take the time to do. I think it was her simplicity that attracted all workers to her. She was gregarious. Also she was sympathetic, always willing to lend an ear, as she had to me once and which remained open on other occasions – a hallmark of psychologists, I think. She'd have been a good one, that's for sure. Your daughter was a helper, I'm sure you know that. And I'm sure she will be helping us still. I feel grateful to have known her. I'll see you later, Rebs!"

Somehow, sitting cross-legged on my bed with all of the notes and messages, many from people that I had never met before that day, but who fiercely loved Rebekah, as I read them, each and every one, it helped. Tears were streaming down my face and sometimes I would have to set aside the letter or card to blow my nose and wipe my face, but hearing the heartfelt expressions of love and loss let me know I was not alone in my suffering.

Others had loved and valued and treasured her too. And they were looking for ways to reach out, caress broken-hearted friends and family, and I was so very, very grateful.

◌ *Rebekah's Journal* ◌

I don't even know where this originated, but last year I made it my goal to say before I got out of bed each morning, "I give myself to you God. Let my mouth speak only words for you. Let my feet go only where you lead. Let my eyes only see what you have for me. Let my hands reach out to others in love." It was my goal to say this every day from then on so that I would only do what God had for me. I did really well with this, then I hit England. For some reason, it became a really rebellious period for me. I was completely away from everything that I knew and everyone that knew me...so I let go of that mantra and just did my own thing. I did what I wanted to and not always what was right. But now that I have gotten my senses back, I have gone back to waking with that heart every day...asking God to take control of every part of me. When you go through the day with that attitude, it's such a great blessing.

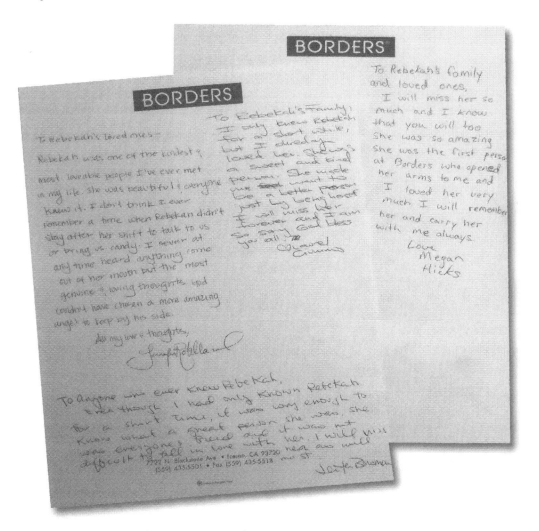

Remembrances from some of Rebekah's co-workers at Borders.

A Thanksgiving Poem

Mom and Dad there is so much to be thankful for...

Cheery faces, cherry pie, and cleansing soap.

Cats, carrots, Christ, and chicken pot pie.

Drive through restaurants and walk-in banks.

Sleep-overs and waking up.

Dining out and staying in.

Horses, hats, harbor seals, and hair.

Hallows on angels, happiness, and healing hearts.

For bright face kindergarteners and wrinkly faced grandparents.

For a wooly blanket and a silk shirt.

For Fridays, family, friends, friendly faces, frogs, and family reunions.

For stories, smiles, summer, seals, "Sam"ta Claus, and sunsets.

For good days and bad days.

For movies, money, metaphors , and Mom's.

For love, laughter, life, and Lynus.

And most of all for all you are and all you do for me.

Love,

Rebekah

Food

We got a call from my brothers, asking if they could take us out to eat. We conferred and selected a favorite restaurant that would shelter us in a private corner. We called to make the reservations. Sam and I had to count again and again, one of us holding up fingers while the other called out the names in order to be sure we had accounted for everyone. We got the giggles over our inability to arrive at the same number with any certainty but we finally got everyone accounted for and the reservation made.

Encased in a leather booth with candle light flickering and family gathered around the huge table, I was able to sit back and just listen to the voices around me. Sara prodded Caleb into doing his spot-on impersonation of the sharks at the support group meeting in *Finding Nemo*. That had us all laughing.

Our meals were served and it was the first time that I really ate a meal since the news. I ate very slowly, looking around the table like someone coming out from under a very strong anesthetic. But these were all adored, familiar faces and voices that meant only comfort and love. I felt peace begin to settle on me. It was a weary peace, and it came gently.

∽ *Rebekah's Journal* ∾

I even keep a quote journal and whenever I am reading, watching TV and movies, or even in conversation: if I hear something that means something to me, I write it down.

I look back on those quotes quite often and they remind me where I have been and how far I have come (or back-tracked). It's like the Bible verses and songs that we love... they reflect how we were at the time that we loved them and they meant something deep to us.

22

Descent into Darkness

I fell asleep easily when we got home, weary and worn, but later, when Sam came to bed I woke up. I gasped for breath as if I had been under water for a long time. I had been dreaming and the images of horror and bloody mangling began to replay in my mind. I had not been haunted by fear in my waking moments but it lurked, just below the surface of conscious thought, and it had broken through on me now.

As I lay in the dark, trying hard not to disturb Sam so he could get rest, I tried to still my racing heart and the sordid images that flickered through my mind. There was nothing of substance but instead lurking, menacing shadows. I could hear the echoes of the yowls and yammers of predatory voices that must have been haunting my dreams. Shrouded in darkness, I could feel them descending on me. I felt their hot breath against my skin and the clamor rose as they sank their fangs into my body, tearing my flesh. I tried to tell myself it was nonsense, all a dream, but the sensation of pain was so real I wondered if the blood would soon begin to flow. I tried to nestle next to Sam, willing myself to resist this nightmarish sensation. I held on to his arm as I struggled beneath the milling hyena mob that yapped and howled for their turn at me.

"Honey, you're hurting me," Sam whispered.

Unbeknownst to me, I had been digging my nails into his arm.

"Sorry," I replied, loosening my grip and sliding under the teeth and claws of my attackers.

I groaned, trying to huddle near to Sam. "Lord," I whispered. "you are my strength and my shield, my strong deliverer."

In the darkness the mob still surrounded me, their triumphant, hideous laughter filling my ears. Claws were tearing away at me and the pain burned within me.

An image rose in my mind. I had seen a wildlife program where hyenas were attacking a pride of lions, trying to kill the cubs. Suddenly, out of the darkness a male lion had emerged. His mane bristled with rage and he scattered the hyenas with a sweep of his huge paw, roaring his anger to the startled pack and slinging them right and left.

"Lion of Judah, Lion of Judah," I cried, my voice disappearing in the night. "Who have I on earth but you? My rock, my fortress, in whom I am safe. Shelter me, Lord. Rescue me," I panted, feeling the mob milling around me.

"I cry out from the depths," I moaned, longing to catch sight of light or rescue."I lift up my head to see my God, striding on the mountaintops," I said, trying to do just that and lift my head. "Who shall I fear? None can make me afraid, if you are near. Oh, Lord, you release me from the hunter's snare. You cause me to rise and take shelter under the shadow of your wings. Shelter me and guard my way."

I felt surrounded by a barren wasteland, darkness on every side and glowing, murderous eyes hovered over me. I felt like a baby gazelle, helpless, and paralyzed with fear. I knew that I was completely powerless to rise or defend myself. I was dead meat on my own.

Yet even as I prayed, I could feel the darkness receding. The melee was being contained. A light and a wholesome presence invaded my own darkness and fear was put to flight. The devilish, taunting laughter ceased and the cruel slashing teeth could find no hold on me.

A sheen of sweat covered me as I came slowly to myself. My labored breathing returned to normal and I was able to sit up.

"Are you alright?" Sam asked.

"Yes," I assured him. "I guess I must have been half asleep but such terror overwhelmed me. I felt like there were real attackers, ripping and biting me. They were laughing and speaking horror. They brought images of death and ruin, destruction and pain. They wanted to drag me into their inky depths and torture me with ugly fearful thoughts."

"I was praying," Sam said. "I knew I could not protect you, and I knew you were being attacked. I heard you calling for the Lion of Judah and I thought of that program where the lion killed those hyenas. I was praying that He would come and rescue you."

"And He did," I said. "I felt smothered and buried by a violent mob, unable to rise or protect myself and without hope."

"I could see it too," Sam said. "Somehow, you were surrounded and I could not get to you."

"From the depths of my soul I cried out to God and He answered and saved me," I said.

"It was like standing on the edge of a battle field, hearing the shriek and concussion of bombs falling," Sam said. "I've been praying for you for over an hour as you struggled and writhed and cried out."

"It's like one of those scenes in the Bible," I said. "where the angel armies encamp around about. Lord, please set your angels round about us and keep our perimeter secure. We need your protection so desperately."

Huddled together, we talked into the night, slowly drifting into peaceful sleep.

❧ *Rebekah's Journal* ❧

Sometimes I amaze myself with the beauty I can create. Tonight I sat for many hours and made collages. No real reason other than I felt like it and I was sending out some letters so I thought that I would make collages specific to those people. It's actually quite fun. You get to dissect their personality and put it on a page in a jumble of pictures and words. Creating an 8 1/2 by 11 movie of someone's life.

I often wonder how people view me. If someone did this for me what would the pictures be? what words would they use to describe me? I almost feel that my collage would be half light, half dark. so bright in parts, but dark and broken in others. The bipolarity of my personality.

what would you put together for mine?

How do you view your own?

*"...He knows
the way I take.*

*When He
has tried me,
I shall come forth
as gold..."*

Our Reasonable Worship

My brothers and their wives came over the next morning for worship along with Sara and Caleb and Missy. We did not feel up to going to formal church service. I had a worship CD playing and I sat, silent and thoughtful, tears streaming once again. Soon we began blending our voices with the songs and then we turned off the music and Jerry read scriptures and talked about the goodness of God.

My sister shared a verse from Job 23:8-12, "Behold, I go forward but He is not there, and backward, but I cannot perceive Him; When He acts on the left, I cannot behold Him; He turns on the right, I cannot see Him. But He knows the way I take; When He has tried me, I shall come forth as gold. My foot has held fast to His path; I have kept His way and not turned aside. I have not departed from the command of His lips. I have treasured the words of His mouth more than my necessary food."

The verses resonated within me. I felt blind with grief, unable to see or follow. The "battle" of the night before still echoed within me and I knew how vulnerable I was. But the phrase "He knows the way I take" spoke such encouragement to me. I felt like a wasteland wanderer, stumbling about in the dark. But as long as God could keep track of me and not let me wander off, it was going to be okay.

We had a communion service together with grape juice and bread. As we were preparing for it, Sam shared from his heart. "I had never, ever really thought about it," he said, "but today, I said, Dear God I am so sorry for YOUR loss! From one father to another, I understand the cost a whole lot more."

We all partook of the communion elements thoughtfully and solemnly.My sister and sisters-in-law somehow opened our fridge and prepared a banquet with lasagna and salad and tons of desert selections. Much of it was from the reception lovingly prepared by the ladies at our church and then sent home wrapped and ready for any need. I marveled at the sweetness and generosity of those women. Their care cushioned and helped us in ways they could not even imagine.

After our meal, my brothers and their wives prepared to leave. Judie, my sister, was staying until after the graveyard service which would be Tuesday because of the Martin Luther King holiday the next day. I was so grateful for their loving presence and told them to thank their children and grandchildren who had sent such sweet words of love and caring.

Caleb and Missy and Sara lingered and we had gentle conversations and more than enough to eat. I sent pies with my brothers and with Caleb and Sara when they left because we could have opened a Marie Callender's outlet with all of the goodies we still had on hand.

∽ *Rebekah's Journal* ∽

Favorite worship song(s): "Heart of worship" has been one of my favorite worship songs for the longest time because it reminds people that what matters isn't making a big show out of your relationship with God, but instead that you just need to go to Him with a willing heart and speak to Him with truth, not with what people think you should say and what they think that you should do. It is about you and God, not about you, God, and everyone else in the world. When you find out why that song was written, it's even more powerful. A man in England wrote it. The church where he was the music minister was very caught up in just the idea of "worship" and had the idea that the only way that you can worship is through music. So they completely cut out the music at the church for a while. During that time, the music minister wrote "Heart of worship." When they started having music again, that was the first song that was sung.

"Love Song" is another song that deeply touches me because it reminds you of how much God loves you. Every time I hear it, I always think about my definition of love and how I measure it. In comparison to God's love, mine is so weak and so limited. God would do anything for us and has done everything for us. I know that we all try to love, but I don't think that we could ever compare to how He loves. So humbling.

A Holiday

Martin Luther King Day and I went and gathered the paper and saw that the commentary that I had written six days earlier was indeed printed.

I had written a guest editorial Tuesday January 13, 2004 — Rebekah's last day on planet earth. But of course, I was happily innocent of that fact when I wrote it. She was the very person that I sent it to for opinion and feedback.

Here is the article as published in the Visalia Times Delta on January 19, 2004.

King Understood Hope

GUEST COMMENTARY • *By Rona Swanson*

Martin Luther King Jr. understood hope. He looked from far away on a promised land where America lived up to its ideals and all men recognized that we are not only created equal but should all have the freedom to pursue our lives with the same vigor and opportunity.

Martin Luther King Jr. knew a lot about hope. It is the fuel that powers our vision and keeps dreams alive. It is the pixie dust to hearts worn down with seemingly vain effort. It is the sunlight gleaming through the clouds.

Our world is in a dark and stormy time. Terror stalks those who love and cherish freedom. Divisive speech and discourteous banter abounds. Cynicism is the order of the day, and the gentle voice of kindness and reason is drowned out by the angry and profane. Hope, that beacon that guides us on to a brighter tomorrow, is needed today. Hope that will lighten the hearts and refuel the souls of all those who are laboring for freedom's fulfillment is needed here.

Did you know that God has a recipe for hope?

The Bible says "we know that suffering produces perseverance.

Perseverance, character... and character, hope."

Actually, this might be more of a science project than a recipe. It is an experiment in progressive reaction as the first element moves through a metamorphosis into the finished project. Funny thing that hope, that sparkling diamond that lightens all hearts, begins with the dreary experience of suffering. But then the by-product of suffering is perseverance, hanging in there and enduring, and that produces character, and character lived out in a human life produces hope.

No wonder Martin Luther King Jr. could speak of hope. He was acquainted with suffering, yet he had resisted embitterment and hate, he had persevered and so his character had been molded and tempered in the fires of ignorance and injustice. He could speak with authority about hope because he had stayed with the experiment through the process and his suffering had led to the beautiful ability to see a better day with such clarity that he could stand at the Lincoln Memorial and see a promised land.

"I have a dream," he said, "that my four children will one day live in a nation where they will not be judged by the color of their skin but the content of their character. I have a dream that one day little black boys and little black girls will be able to join hands with little white boys and little white girls and walk together as sisters and brothers. This is the faith with which I return to the South. With this faith we will be able to hew out of the mountain of despair a stone of hope."

As we remember Martin Luther King Jr., let's honor his vision and renew his dream.

Let us vow to become color-blind and character-savvy. As brothers and sisters, we need to nurture and encourage those who are struggling.

We can cheer them on and teach them that character only comes to those who persevere. And we must remember that character is to be prized and fed and nourished and appreciated because without the production of character and the existence of that quality, hope fails.

The character of Americans has always been one of adventurers, dreamers, explorers. In dark days when the whole world was threatened, the "Yanks" became the hope of the world. Perhaps we can allow Dr. King to renew in us our resolve to focus on the dream and make character the value we prize. The harvest of hope for the future will be bright indeed.

Subj: Re: Letter to the Editor
Date: 1/13/04 11:58:25 AM Pacific Standard Time
From: Bekahfluterby
To: RONASAM

Very good. :) God's recipe for hope is an interesting one. Something that most people do not see and do not want to go through you. Great job as always. This is why people love you. You are a beacon of light they can always count on. :)
Love,
Beck

Rebekah and I talked on the phone that day, planned a shopping excursion to a used book store for a long list of classics she needed for an advanced lit course she was participating in. We talked about the whole idea of suffering and how God uses the very agony and struggle to develop our character. She liked my allusion to the "sparkling diamond" since we were both fans of Moulin Rouge, and I laughed at her lively, never-miss-a-thing mind.

As I sat in my living room staring at the paper and remembering our conversation, I realized how much God had had me preaching to my own self.

Could I trust Him to bring HOPE from the universe of suffering that I was going through?

I did not know how He could produce good from the pain that I felt. I was weary and the weight of losing Rebekah felt bone-crushing, but I closed the paper and closed my eyes and prayed, "I am trusting you, God...I am trusting you."

⌒ *Rebekah's Journal* ⌒

I have read "Our Town" many times. After the people die they can choose to go back and be among the living again. They don't so much hear what everyone else is thinking, but they know what the outcome of everything will be. They know that people will die in tragic accidents, etc. It's such a profound book. But the thing they say is...don't choose any day that was too important because it will hurt too much.

I'd want to choose a truly happy day. I'd choose a day in my childhood where I was out horseback riding with my mom and brother. I would probably be reciting, as I often did when I was a child, "when I was 35, I liked to cook. When I was 50, I had lots of cats." I guess I really did do that (who knows why) and it was great entertainment for my mom. Jedi (our horse) would probably abruptly stop a few times to eat a thistle and Babe (another horse of ours) would be as sweet and patient as ever. I guess it was days like those that really shaped me. Who knew that a girl who grew up in such a podunk town would have such a raging passion and desire to see the world? Go figure.

Where will I be 10 years from now? I don't know, but at this point all I can say is where God wants me to be.

it's actually a good place to be. Right now I just get to float and live life. I don't know what direction I am going to go so I just get to sit and wait for him to send me one way or another down the stream.

Ten years from now...I HOPE to be married. I don't think that God would give me this desire if he wasn't going to fulfill it. I plan on working in whatever mission field I am in, whether that be my job or a foreign country or my job in a foreign country. I plan to be using English in whatever I do. It really is my passion in life and I am so glad that it's my major. Other than that, I am up for suggestions!

oh and I will be living with my basset hound/beagle named Waldo, of course. :)

Gray and Gentle Day

My sister Judie and I took advantage of the holiday and drove up into the foothills. The day was gray and foggy. Our brothers had gone up to Sequoia National Park on Saturday while Judie arranged and re-arranged all of the food and I read through the cards and letters after the service. They had said how beautiful it was and showed us pictures of them by a snowy General Sherman tree and the valley below at sunset. I did not have the energy to go all of the way up to the park but we had lunch at a Mexican restaurant in the little town of Three Rivers and we got to listen to the water running and see a little bit of scenery.

It was nice to just sit, my sister and I, and talk as if nothing unusual at all was going on. I welcomed it, fully aware that I would not forget my agony or slip the grip of such sorrow soon.

When we arrived back home, every surface was filled with flowers and plants. The funeral home had delivered the arrangements and plants that had been sent. Judie and I spent gentle hours gazing at the extravagant beauty of the flowers that now perfumed our home.

∞ *Rebekah's Journal* ∞

Jackie and I finally explored the Park today. I love our campus! We went and sat down by the pond for a while (it's pretty darn big). There are swans and ducks! They are so beautiful. :)

Now I am sitting in my room with the windows open. There is a lush breeze blowing through currently with a magnificent sunset outside of my window. Fingers of pink and purple are stretching across the sky. Reaching across the heavens into the clouds still bursting with light. The wind is blowing the clouds across the sky. The heavens are bursting with life.

It's sad how quickly it fades. The sky is now filled with dark purples and blues, along with patches of light blue. The trees are dancing, seemingly rejoicing in the fresh breeze. There is an intricate dance going on between the wind and the trees. And once again the night is alive, the ducks and swans are letting out their last calls (I can hear them through my window) and the world is growing quiet, yet makes me feel so very alive and in love all over again.

*an entry from Rebekah's Journal
while she was in England

The Burial

As we pulled up at the cemetery for the graveside service, there in the middle of the drive was Tom, a client of mine. He was a huge black man who had been married to his itty-bitty little white wife Ruth. Ruth had passed away a few months earlier and I had been there at her funeral and afterwards to walk him through the process of life insurance claims. There stood Tom, his big legs braced and looking as solid as a Redwood tree.

I ran up to him and he wrapped me in a bear hug. "Don't you worry now, Rona," he said. "My Ruth is going to show her the ropes!"

I leaned back and looked into his precious face and laughed. "Tom," I shouted. "I know God takes care of us, but I am so glad that He gives us flesh and blood friends to be beside us when we lose our loved ones. It makes all of the difference!"

He patted my hand as we walked to the canopy and the stand where the coffin would be placed. I sat down in the place reserved for me. Missy and Sara and Judie were with me as well.

People began to gather. The pallbearers were all there, dressed in their suits.

My husband Sam, his brilliant humor shaded with such sorrow and loss.

Caleb, big brother, bearing himself with such strength and love.

Bill, our precious buddy, who just a few weeks before had laughed and celebrated the New Year with Sam and Rebekah and I as we had a *Band of Brothers* marathon at our home.

Alex, who had once been my secretary years ago and had gone on to become a teacher. He had been Rebekah's favorite teacher in her senior year of high school. She reveled in the challenges of his AP government class and had been inspired to actively form and express political opinion and policy under his loving encouragement.

Dennis, Rebekah's youth pastor and the one who had been so supportive of her as she grew into young adulthood.

Richard, a friend from when she was just a little girl. He shared cherished memories of the young girl who, even at age seven, had ideas and advice that impacted his life. Richard and Caleb and Rebekah had all three been baptized in a celebration on the same night.

The back of the hearse opened and the metallic blue coffin emerged and the men carried her to her final resting place. When they were done and had taken their seats, Mike Hand spoke about a life well lived and the confidence that we all shared that we would see her again.

All of Rebekah's college friends were there with yellow long-stemmed roses that they placed on the coffin.

While we were standing and talking and greeting the people who had come, Mike told me that indeed, Ken had come to the service on Saturday. We had not had any idea that he had been present because Mike and Bill had devised a plan to be on the lookout. When he did arrive, he was seated with his wife in the back of the auditorium and they placed ushers intentionally to block our view of being able to see him when we were escorted to the front row. Then, after the service, we were led to the reception room and Bill followed Ken and his wife to the parking lot.

"I could not forbid them to be there," Mike said, "but we could make sure that they did not disturb you." There had been men who were fully aware of the situation who were prepared to intervene before he could make any kind of a scene.

I was overwhelmed with gratitude at the protective cover we had been afforded by these men who were looking out for us, even while we were so happily innocent of the situation.

The people began to leave and Sam came and took my elbow. I did not want to go. It made no sense but I wanted to stay, to be there, to somehow safeguard or protect or see to the care of Rebekah. It was a raging, animal desire. Emotionally, I could feel a cornered animal, snarling and growling for everyone to back away, to leave me alone. But instead, I placed my hand on the coffin and whispered my love to the one my heart longed for.

Caleb patted the surface as well, his face set and sad.

We went to lunch as a big group. There was laughter and good food and I thanked everyone for being there.

I left to take Judie to the airport to catch her flight home. As we sat in the terminal, the Mercy Me song *I Can Only Imagine* was playing over the speakers. I smiled, remembering Rebekah's tear-streaked face as we sang it together and she said, "Oh, Mom, I'm gonna dance!" Was she dancing even now?

Hugs and tears and Judie was gone from us.

I stopped at a store on the way home to buy cards so that I could send notes of thanks to all who had reached out to us.

When I got home, Sam, Sara, Caleb and Missy were there. Sara had asked if "just us" could gather and watch *Finding Nemo* once it was all over. I slipped upstairs to change and when I came down I said, "Listen up! I have something really important to say!"

Caleb had been lying down on the couch, half asleep.

He sat upright and fixed his eyes on me.

"You know, Rebekah used to always say that when I got old and feeble, she would wipe the drool from my mouth," I said with a smile. "So I need to know which one of you will step up and take over!"

Caleb and Sara laughed — just little laughs — but it was laughter.

We watched the movie, or semi-watched the movie, or dozed through the movie, but it was another day that we walked through together.

∽ *Rebekah's Journal* ∽

Note from Mom:

"of course I hope you know that you are missed and loved in abundance. You are such a precious presence that not having you around is VERY noticeable...kind of like the sun when we have a string of foggy days. Any little glimpse of the sun's rays cheers the heart and we practically go crazy when we get blue sky and untainted access to the sunlight."

Sometimes the world lets you know that you're special. ☺

*an entry from Rebekah's Journal
while she was in England

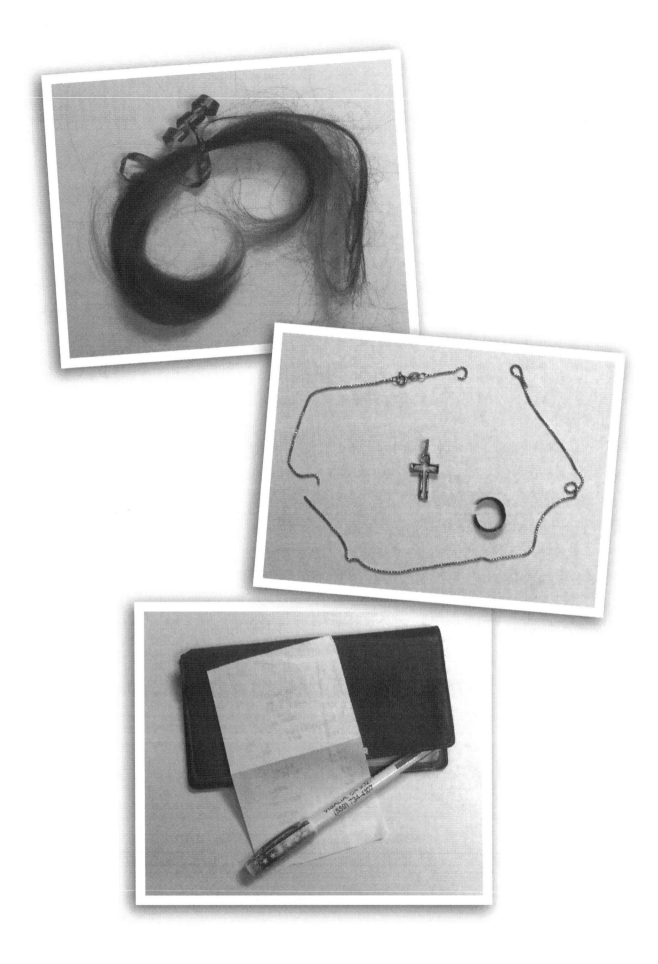

Coming to Grips

Our friend Cecilia insisted that we take a week away from our business, so she came and babysat our insurance office so we would not have to worry about anything at all.

We went back to the funeral home in order to pay our bill and make arrangements for the headstone. They also had Rebekah's personal effects that had been bagged and traveled with her from morgue to donor center to the funeral home.

I could see her purse through the clear plastic bag. Steve also assured me that he had included the lock of hair as well. Hunger is the only way to describe what I felt... ravenous hunger to be alone and to touch her things. We concluded our business while I hugged the package to my chest and, once home, I climbed the stairs to our room and sat down on the bed. I opened the bag and pulled out Beck's purse. It was soiled. There were two plastic bags inside. One was clear and held a lengthy lock of my girl's hair. The other had a label and writing and as I opened it to examine the contents and the paper. I realized it was a receipt from the coroner's office for all of the items of value in the purse. It listed a blue cloth wallet with a VISA and a debit card. Also listed was the check book with checks #1023 – 1030. Finally it showed a toe ring with stars and a necklace with a cross with the notation – damaged. I tipped the bag up and let the contents fall into my hand. Her necklace, the cross still whole and intact, but the chain sliding out in three separate portions. I opened her wallet and her driver's license and student card smiled up at me. There was a tube of lip gloss and a tube of Burt's Bee's lip balm.

I ran my hand over the check book and remembered Rebekah sharing with me a story from right before Christmas break. They were cramming for finals, and she had offered to make a Taco Bell run for food. She had gone inside to order and was walking back out to the parking lot. She had noticed a couple with an OUT OF WORK sign beside the sidewalk but really hadn't paid much attention. Now, as she was approaching them again, she saw a group of young teenage boys beside them. One of the boys spit right in the man's face. The others were laughing. As they walked on, the man ran his sleeve across his face and said, "God, bless them" as Rebekah was passing by. She said it almost made her knees give out, hearing that man bless boys who had been so completely full of hate and venom. Her mind raced to think what she could do. First, she thought she would take them to buy some groceries but quickly discarded the idea, knowing I would NOT want her driving around with unknown strangers in her car. So she turned around and said, "Let me buy you dinner!"

The man and woman followed her inside. They were going to split a taco and a drink but Rebekah would not hear of it, insisting that they both have their own meal and preferred drink. While they were waiting, the man told Rebekah that they had come to Fresno because they were promised a job but it did not come through. "This is not us," he kept saying, "This is not us."

Rebekah paid for their meal, got them comfortably seated in a booth and told them again and again that they were welcome because the man would not stop thanking her. She had shown me the receipt for $6.74. "I keep this here in my checkbook register," she explained. "So that anytime I get to feeling sorry for myself as a poor college kid, I can look at this and remember how good I have it!"

I rubbed the vinyl cover of her checkbook, remembering the sparkle in her eyes as she spoke of the privilege of buying a meal for that couple. I remembered her describing the horror of watching him spit upon and then the heart-melting wonder when she heard him praying for those who had done it. I remembered it all and slid all of the treasures back into the purse and held it to my chest, rocking and weeping. I can hold the very items that were there with her at the very last...but I cannot hold her. This is a hunger and a scream of need that goes unanswered. Like a live nerve, it sends shock waves through me, and all I can do is cry.

We arranged with Rebekah's roommates to drive up to her college and collect her things. It was so sweet to see the blue containers that they had purchased, and with hugs and kisses, we loaded the things and brought them home. I put all of the containers in the middle of the living room and began opening them one by one. Some contained household goods – pots and pans, bedding, towels – but then there were the ones that had personal items and the greatest treasure of all, her journals. I set them lovingly aside and began to slowly put things away, bit by bit. All of my movements were slow. It was as if the very atmosphere had grown dense. To pick something up or carry something to another room took such effort, it felt like I was wearing gravity boots.

I was finally able to move the remaining things into Rebekah's room upstairs, but I had a promise for the next day.

The power company had left a notice earlier in the week that we would have no power for a few hours the next day. I was delighted because there would be no disturbances, no distractions and I could sit and read journals all day long.

∞ *Rebekah's Journal* ∞

Cried out

I cried out to God today,
in despair.
As all the frustrations piled up,
one by one.
I felt overcome by them.
utterly helpless
against the pain they caused.
Drained by the day's events.
Devoid of all feeling,
except weakness.
I wanted to lay there
in the sweet expanses
of the day
and know that I would be safe.
To know that there was no more pain
to be felt.
That there were no more tears
to be shed.
That I could go on with new energy
provided by Him.
I know that moment of realization
will come, but it is yet to reach me.

Baby Rebekah in my arms..

Lost in Memories

I spent the day reading and reading and reading. I laughed and cried and laughed some more. In the front of her latest journal was a card from me:

> Dear Rebekah,
>
> Pastor Guerra asked us last Saturday "What do you want to teach your children?" Here it is – TRUST IN THE LORD WITH ALL YOUR HEART – DON'T COUNT ON YOUR LIMITED UNDER-STANDING. IN EVERYTHING, CONSULT HIM FIRST AND HE WILL DIRECT YOUR PATH.
>
> There are so many things I could tell you (and do!) but most of all – there is a blessed reunion planned – the final homecoming! I'll probably get there first, but I'm saving a place for you!
>
> I love you SO much — more than can be measured!
>
> Mom

I remembered writing that card September 4 of 2003. I had felt so challenged to try to put into words what I wanted my children to know.

My own mother had passed away from cancer when I was only 10. I was the youngest child and the one thing I had longed for my entire life was a mother's advice. So I wanted it to be available to my own children.

It had been years earlier, on my 42nd birthday, when I was confessing to everyone what a relief it was to make it past the age that my own mother had died, that I discovered how such knowledge had impacted Rebekah, my youngest. She confessed that she had prayed and prayed that I would live and not leave her alone as a little girl. We hugged and laughed about our own private worries and Caleb said, "You're looking healthy enough Mom. I think you're good for another year or two!" I punched him on the shoulder, and we went back to everyday chatter.

Now as I leaned back against the cushions of the love seat, I marveled at the way that God had entwined my heart with Rebekah's.

My mother had died in January as well. January 16, 1966. It seemed somewhat profound that all of my siblings had gathered once again in January for a funeral together. Mother's loss had been shattering to us all. Judie and Jerry were both married with children. Rod was in high school. I was the little kid.

Dad did not really know what to do and so, in three months, he remarried and moved me and my new "mom" to a different city. Everything that had been familiar, everything of Mother, was out of sight and we moved on. I was a kid, what did I know?

It wasn't until six years later, when my step-mother was dying of cancer and my best friend and her sister asked me, "What is it like to have your mother die?"

It was an innocent enough question.

They were not rude strangers, but my most intimate friends.

I never expected the force of the bursting dam of grief when I actually tried to answer their question. I began sobbing uncontrollably. It frightened them and they felt terrible. It wasn't their fault. I had just been waiting six years to actually mourn my mother's death. It was not pretty when I let it out. Now, I told myself that I could have as much time as I needed, I could cry as much as I wanted, I could look at Rebekah's pictures and things as often as I wanted to. There was no rush to "move on" or "get past" anything.

I knew, instinctively, that the agony of losing her would take a miracle in order to recover. I also knew it would not be an overnight process, so I slowly, gently, gave myself permission to read in silence all through the day.

Sam reminded me that people do need food, so I got up and had a meal but the day was spent lost in memories and reflections.

Like this one from August 2003:

∽ *Rebekah's Journal* ∽

It was so odd tonight. I sat for hours around a table with my mom, step-dad, and my sister and her boyfriend, and my brother and his fiancée. Yet, I didn't feel like the oddball out, the only person that was alone.

I sat there instead watching my family interact. For the first time in my adult life, we were all together outside the bubble of my parent's house. Everyone's chosen life partner was there (except of course — mine — who hasn't been chosen yet).

For the first time it hit me, it really hit me that both Sara and Caleb have lives that I don't know all about now. They would both talk with their significant other about things I didn't have any knowledge of, then tell us tidbits or laugh at their own inside jokes. This isn't allowed. They aren't supposed to have their own outside life that I don't know about.

Yes, I know that I have mine. I know I have experience that no one knows about and that only a few ever will find out about, but it's ok for me to have this outside life.

It's just not ok for them!

Growing up, my brother and I were so close. We were best friends. Now we are grown up. He's getting married. I still don't quite cope with it. He is always supposed to be my brother. Every Christmas we are all supposed to climb down the stairs in slipper socks and with sleepy eyes to unwrap the presents as a family. My mom, brother, and I are supposed to savor hot cinnamon rolls together on Christmas morning. That's the way it's supposed to be. It's all changing.

Tonight I saw that. I really saw it for the first time. In 9 months I am going to be a college graduate. In 9 months, I will have a job that isn't meant to last just for a summer. I am really an adult now. How do I act like one?

I laughed as I read the entry. I remembered the barbeque well and Rebekah's interest in everyone and everything.

Little sis had become accomplished traveler, speaker, and soon to be graduate with a double degree. She had learned to articulate so very well her love and appreciation of others and her surroundings. She continued to stretch herself with more and more studies, tackling a new literature course with hefty reading. Actually, we were both looking forward to that because we would read and discuss the books together so we had our own private little book club and it was wonderful.

She was so honest and open about her own progress, her own thoughts and struggles that she welcomed others to share as well.

This was an essay from her senior year in high school. When the year kicked off, her AP teacher had asked for an essay on what the student would die for. This was her reply.

Rebekah Swanson
Period 5
September 15, 1999

"What I Would Die For" Essay

In this day it is far too often that you hear people say, "I would die for that dress" or "This dessert is to die for" but the question is, how many of these people would truly lay down their life for a dress or a dessert? People seem to take the concept of death lightly and no longer understand the meaning of those words that they utter countless times a day. But what would you die for? That is the real question. As I search my soul for the answer, I see that the response is obvious. I would die for my beliefs.

Since I was a young girl, I have believed in Jesus Christ and have learned each day about His never-ending love for me. As I was taught these things, He became a huge part of my life. Now I live in the Word and hunger for God's presence in my life each day to lead me down the path that He has chosen for me. As I immerse myself in God's presence, I see that life would not exist without Him. God created all that is and gave us life on this earth. Without Him, there would be nothing.

From my perspective, the thought of laying down my life for the cause of Christ is not so large a price. I believe that this life, the life lived in the flesh, is but a short foretaste of my "real" life. God has created eternal souls for all of us and the simple surrender of life in my body would not be too high a price.

Before you begin to think that I am some sort of religious whacko who is going to don the Nikes and drink the "special" Kool-Aid the next time a relative of Hale Bopp comes round the bend, I just want to say that I am not planning to die for anything.

My desire is to LIVE for God. However, when asked what I would die for, I can think of no greater treasure than my faith.

My belief in Jesus Christ is the thing that starts and ends my every day. As I wake up in the morning I pray to God to be with me throughout the day and give me strength. At the end of the day, I thank Him for all of the blessings that He has bestowed on me. God is the beginning and the end of each day for me and will be with me from the beginning to the end of my life.

———————

There was so much to read, and I soaked in her thoughts and beliefs.

Like the acronym tucked away in a notebook based on her name:

✑ *Rebekah's Journal* ✑

R   Real life is supposed to be enjoyed

E   Even when we are

B   Breaking over the past mistakes

E   Everyone makes – including us.

K   Kids never believe they will do something

A   As stupid as their parents.

H   How our words can bite us in the ass.

———————

I laughed out loud at that one.

We don't yet see things clearly. We're squinting in a fog, peering through a mist. But it won't be long before the weather clears and the sun shines bright! We'll see it all then, see it all as clearly as God sees us, knowing him directly just as he knows us! But for right now, until that completeness, we have three things to do to lead us toward that consummation: Trust steadily in God, hope unswervingly, love extravagantly. And the best of the three is love.

— *1 Corinthians 13:12-13 (The Message)*

Try to Return

The weekend came and went. Sam played on the worship team at church, and I made it through the service, weeping gently as we sang worship songs.

Everyone wanted to come and hug us, let us know they were praying for us.

It was good to feel those hugs but hard to present ourselves in public. Everything in me felt ill-equipped for conversation or contact, so we had to force ourselves to endure the attention until we could return home. The last thing we wanted was anyone's notice. All we were longing for was a return to normal.

I told my sister that I had come to the conclusion that our pain was not something that we would slog through over the weekend with grit teeth.

This would be more of a marathon effort.

There is such a panicked feeling to want to run from the sorrow, to throw it off and be rid of it. To banish it from thought or emotion.

But there was also the longing, the desire, to think so tenderly of Rebekah.

So I realized that we would have to make friends with this companion of grief. I would need to learn how to walk the road with it, allowing it permission to speak.

Yet I also knew that I could not force other travelers on the road to be burdened by my personal sorrow.

God, dear God, give me grace to walk or crawl or somehow navigate forward.

❧ *Rebekah's Journal* ❧

Today is the best kind of anniversary. One month ago, I started my love affair with England. For one month, it has never let me down. It has held me in its bosom and wrapped me in its arms of sunrays and wind every morning and evening.

I'm in love and it's the best kind of love. It's a love made of longing that is fulfilled every day and night. A love that never goes unanswered. A love that is always fresh with the promise of new discovery and fulfilled with romance and whispered promises in the trees.

Each morning I will be awakened by sunbeam kisses and each night silver moon rays will tuck me in.

I fall in love with the world a little more each day and I never want it to end. Falling in love has never been this good.

Rebekah sliding down a hand rail in London (above) and enjoying France (right).

Back to Work

Sam and I returned to our office.

We were both so fragile that we were thankful to have one another.

The phone rang and soon there were requests for copies of policies and new cars that needed to be added to coverage. We quickly fell into the swing of things.

Then Sam transferred a call to me and when I picked up, a women's wailing voice came through.

"I need to come and meet with you," she said.

"About what?" I asked.

"I need to come and grieve with you," she explained.

She began explaining who she was. Our children had been in high school together. "I know what you are going through," she sobbed. "I need to come and grieve with you. I lost a child four years ago. I need to get you connected with my grief therapy group."

"I am so sorry," I replied. "I cannot meet with you today. This is my first day back in my office and I am doing my very best to just keep a clear and focused head to take care of business."

"But I need to grieve with you," she moaned.

"I am so sorry, but I cannot meet with you," I answered. My racing mind was thinking that if she was in this rough of shape after four years, I did not want an introduction to her group grief therapy either!

"You have to let it out," she urged. "Let me come and grieve beside you."

"I cannot," I replied firmly. "I need to go now because I have lots of things that I must accomplish today. Thank you for your concern," I added in parting.

As I was placing the receiver down, she wailed loudly, "I want an insurance quote!"

I placed the phone gently in the cradle, unnerved with the raw, hungry desire to somehow get to my presence.

Sam came to the doorway of my office and asked if I was okay. I told him about the conversation and he said, "I think we'll file that under the heading of help we don't need today!"

AMEN!

Unholy and unrestrained grief can make the griever almost vampirish in their need for fresh blood to revive the agony. I realized with a shudder that I needed to be guarded and prepared. Somehow the newness of our pain made us desirable to those who fed on such things.

∞ *Rebekah's Journal* ∞

Home sickness hits at the worst times. Like now. Almost one and I have to be up at eight for a full day of lectures. This too while I am sick. Yet, I can't stop crying and I can't stop wishing for nothing more than a hug from my mom.

Mom: "If I had to choose who gets to go for fun...it would always be you. If I get to choose who would swallow hardship or pain, I would always go first...but I think that is what Mommy love is...and God plants it in your heart. You'll see one day".

*an entry from Rebekah's Journal
while she was in England

Computer

Among the things that came home from college with us was Rebekah's laptop.

I found myself listening to her music and reading her papers and journal entries. So much, so much of her essence and joy and frankness was contained there.

I could get lost in it if I let myself but duty calls to rise and answer calls for service and help in our insurance business. So I have learned to schedule time for me to be able to delve into her essence alone.

People tell me I am doing good. I laugh and tell them that if they could see me as I really am emotionally – I would be in a full body cast. Everything hurts. Everything takes tremendous effort and focus

I think grief is like a terrible head injury. At first, you really aren't thinking straight and then, as the fog clears and the numbness begins to recede, you begin to feel all of the places that are broken and hurting. I am so very aware of where it hurts and how bad.

Some days I can barely make it to my car to go home for the evening before the tears start to flow. Poor Sam, there is really nothing that he can do. I told him, "It's okay, I just need to leak regularly from my eyes. It is a pressure outlet".

Sam gets the *Message* version of the Bible and reads out loud to me while I fix dinner. It helps. Sometimes we both have tears streaming, but it's okay. I read somewhere that tears are the body's most powerful way to rid itself of toxins. I told Sam that at this rate, we are going to live to be two hundred years old at least!

My one unchangeable routine is answering the kind cards and notes we have received. I spend time every evening doing just that.

This was my letter to *Borders*:

January 29, 2004

Dear Borders Family,
    I want to thank you all for your wonderful notes and warm hugs and remembrances of Rebekah. I appreciate it so much.
    Rebekah and I were so very close and I miss her very much. I have discovered that my grief is only in wanting more time with her, not some-

thing different. We had such a rich and loving relationship that nothing was left unsaid and I have no regrets.

We are so humbled with the outpouring of love and comfort and support that we have received. Our home looks and smells like a florist shop. Springtime blossoms perfume the air.

Cards and letters and e-mails have come flooding in as a mighty wave of caring. We are so blessed and so rich in the love of friends and family.

We will miss Rebekah in ways and with pain that we are only coming to grasp. That is our challenge – to bravely face and work through such grief. There is, however, not one ounce of sadness regarding Rebekah or where her spirit resides now. We know that she is in joy in the presence of the Savior that she loved so much.

One last thing. In evidence of God's grace. Rebekah had been home for winter break and did not move back to college until Sunday the 11th. Usually she would be up and loading and moving so that she would be back on campus in the early afternoon. That day Rebekah was in no hurry to go. Sam was gone, serving his National Guard weekend.

It was just us girls. I made English tea, coddled eggs, and English Muffins (crumpets) and we watched *Sense and Sensibility* (as an English major and having studied abroad in England last year, she was a HUGE Jane Austen fan). We had a fire in the fireplace and after the movie we just sat and talked. The day was soft and gentle. Caleb, her beloved older brother, just "happened" to stop by with his fiancée Melissa, who is also one of Rebekah's childhood friends. They left after a nice visit and hugs and kisses.

Rebekah still was not in a hurry so we had dinner together and I assisted Rebekah in loading her car. We hugged and she started to climb in her car. Then she came back and said, "One more hug" with her arms thrown wide and we held one another. She whispered in my ear, "I know for a fact that you are the best Mother on the face of the earth."

I replied, "Oh, honey, mommying is easy with a daughter like you."

To which she said, "No, I wouldn't be a daughter like me without a Mom like you."

We teased as she got in the car with me saying, "No, it's you." and she replying, "No, it's You!"

She buckled up and backed out of the drive. She rolled down her window and waved and then blew kisses as she drove away. That was my last physical time with Rebekah although we had talked and e-mailed on Monday and Tuesday.

I marvel at God's goodness. There were no words left unsaid, no doubt how much love we shared and she left many friends and the rest of her family with the same loving picture of the last time they saw Rebekah.

Our grief is huge but only because we do not feel her touch, hear her sweet voice, and experience her presence right now. We know, however, that this is but an intermission...no, really this is just a trivial preview before the feature attraction, and one day we will share the presence of all those who have gone before as we bathe in the perfecting presence of the King of Kings.

Thanks for your love and prayers and support. It means so very much!

Sincerely,

Rebekah's Mom, Rona Swanson

Sometimes I feel like I am living in a continuum where seconds, minutes, hours, even days no longer matter. All that matters anymore is experience.

Take in a deep breath and suck in all the life around you.

Walking to town today, I ran my hand along the tall red, brick wall as I thought to myself about how many times I have passed this wall and how every time I have missed all the many rivets and it's striking character. I pranced through the daffodils and it struck me moment after moment that I won't be able to do this every day that in due time this will no longer be...it will no longer...

Rebekah dancing in Mrs. Curtis' third grade class.

32

Back to School

I had been volunteering in Mrs. Curtis' third grade class since Rebekah had been a student there. Every Thursday morning I would go and read. I wanted to go back and so I did, reading a story like nothing in my life was strange or different. I asked my questions and we had discussion, the way we always did it. I was already out of the room, breathing a sigh of relief at having gotten over that hurdle, when Logan (who is the red-headed disrupter of the class) yelled, "I am SO sorry about your daughter!"

It sorta stopped me in my tracks and I realized that I needed to address that topic with the kids. I thought about going back in but thought better of it, knowing that the next week I would have to cross the bridge of telling them the truth about my loss. As I walked into the room that next Thursday, I told them I did not bring a story to read, but that some stories are written on paper and some stories are written on our hearts.

I showed them pictures of Rebekah and told about her life. I told them that when we moved to Visalia, Rebekah was in the 2nd grade. I said that she was very quiet and shy at that time. Then she entered 3rd grade and guess who her teacher was?

They all shouted, "MRS CURTIS!" and I showed them a picture of Rebekah square dancing in 3rd grade and said, "She sure doesn't look quiet and shy anymore. Mrs. Curtis is a great teacher."

I showed them photos of Rebekah's life, and then explained that she had died in an auto accident on January 13th.

Mrs. Curtis was grabbing tissues out of a box in the back of the room as I continued by reading them an e-mail I had received from my friend Ray.

Dear Rona,
    It has taken me several days to try and think of the right words to express my sympathy to you, and the grief I share for the loss of Rebekah.
    Several years ago, I decided to cancel both newspapers because I was tired of bombarding my senses with all the bad that happens in the world...and the growing tendency to believe that the bad dominates our

existence. The downside of not reading the news is that I don't hear about such tragedies as Rebekah's death until after the services are held, and I am unable to attend. I guess it's a trade-off.

Rebekah was one of the shining lights in our existence that should have given us all optimism – that goodness, and mercy and care and concern for others really do prevail. She showed us that we do have hope, and that we can take the time to care about other people. In a world that has become dominated by FAX machines, cell phones, digital cameras and the speed of the internet, she showed us how to slow down and take the time to show personal concern for our fellow beings.

Years ago, when I was having marital difficulties and I was about as low as I could get, Rebekah took the time to write out about 50 little compliments on little pieces of paper. She then wrapped each one individually in a colored ribbon, put them all in a box, and brought them to me with a note on the box entitled "Happy Medicine - prescribed by Rebekah Swanson". I still have that little box, and I still treasure it...now, more than ever. When I heard of Rebekah's accident, I took out a few of the little scrolls and read them... to remind myself of how a little 13-year-old girl took the time to show another human being how much she cared.

It was wrong for her to go. The world needed Rebekah. We have lost the "personal touch" and she was here to teach us how to get it back. Some of us will die, and that will be it. Others of us can hope that our lives will be meaningful enough that we will leave a legacy that will keep our spirits alive in the hearts of those we leave behind. In Rebekah's case, she will live on...in the kind things she did for others... like the little scrolls of cheer, wrapped in brightly colored ribbons... that lifted the spirits of a sad and grieving man.

Our loss is Heaven's gain.

God bless you. My thoughts and prayers are with you.

In His love,

Ray

Then I pulled out one of my most treasured possessions and showed them MY very own Happy Medicine box prescribed by Dr. Rebekah Swanson. It shows a prescription instruction to take as many as necessary. I have gone to those little scrolls again and again, reading her specific expressions of love. I untied some of the ribbons and read them to the students. I assured them that this was one prescription that you can never overdose on.

An amazing, almost holy time ensued as we discussed life and death and heaven and prayer and God's ability to sustain and hold us. The conversation was amazing and children can ask such frank questions but it was important for them to be able to talk.

As I was preparing to leave, Mrs. Curtis, her nose and eyes red said," I think maybe we should plan to make Happy Medicine boxes for our Moms this Mother's Day, what do you think?"

The classroom erupted and the kids started talking about their commitment to make notes on all of the particularly spectacular characteristics or skills of their Moms. As I walked away from what could have been a devastating time of heartache, I thought, "Ahhh...the torch has been passed and a new generation of light bearers carry the standard."

∽ *Rebekah's Journal* ∽

My favorite teacher would have to be Mrs. Curtis who was my third grade teacher. I had just moved from Glennville to Visalia the year before and I had gone through huge culture shock. I was floundering so much. I had gone from a town of 100 to one of 100, 000. I used to be the big fish in a small pond and now I was a small fish in a big pond.

Then Mrs. Curtis came along. She encouraged me so much. She made me blossom so much. My grades all started going back up and she gave me faith in myself again.

This past February when I was going to England she sent me a card with a picture of a broken fence on it and on the inside wrote, "I thought this card was appropriate for you. Fences often symbolize boundaries and limits, broken fences can represent going beyond imposed limits. I am excited that you are breaking out of the confines of a local education. What a great opportunity for you! When you return I am going to vicariously visit England, the country I have most wanted to see. My thoughts and prayers go with you."

After all these years she is still there...still encouraging me in all that I do. She has been such a blessing throughout my life. :)

FRESNO PACIFIC UNIVERSITY MUSIC DEPARTMENT

Presents

SENIOR TRUMPET RECITAL

JAMES LOOMIS

Trumpet

ARLENE STEFFEN

Piano

WAYNE HUBER

Trumpet Instructor

SUNDAY, FEBRUARY 29, 2004 ~ 3:00 PM

BUTLER AVENUE MENNONITE BRETHREN CHURCH

FRESNO, CA

*This recital is given in partial fulfillment of the requirements for a
Bachelor of Arts Degree in Music, Secondary Teaching Emphasis*

Invitation

We received an invitation to attend Jimmy Loomis' trumpet recital at Fresno Pacific.

Jimmy is a music major and one of Rebekah's 'bestest' pals. I RSVP'd that we would be there and planned to take a gift for each of her friends.

I knew exactly what I wanted to do. When Rebekah was in high school, she had made some masks in art class, each one unique and wonderful. She had hung them around the top of her walls in her room and had tied them all to one another with strands of connecting ribbon. I gently snipped the ribbons between them and took them down. There were seven of them and I placed them in gift bags for each of her friends along with a note from me and a copy of a poem that I had found in her journals.

∽ Rebekah's Journal ∾
(Sometime in 2003)

For many days I have been contemplating this topic...the part about masks intrigued me. why are people so compelled to wear masks to disguise their true being...the true identity that lies within them?

At first glance I thought it was a fear, but a fear of what you may ask...most would think it is a fear of being too small, of being weak, of not being enough for the world.

But that is so far from the truth...it is a fear of being too much, of letting your light shine too bright, of allowing people to really see what depth you hold. it is not a fear of our weakness or darkness but of light and strength. But what creates this? what makes us terrified of our own magnificence? over the years we have lies fed to us, some to bigger extremes than others. we are made to believe that we are worthless, stupid, ugly, any vast number of things...and we get roped into it...believing the lies and losing self worth day by day until you are afraid to show the amazing glory of who you really are and hide behind masks.

People build these masks by believing what's been fed to them and lowering themselves to that level...getting into drinking or drugs, debasing themselves by going out and having sex with every member of the opposite sex (or to be pc every member of their sexual preference) or even stooping as low as making those around you feel low or beating the crud out of those you are supposed to care about. In a battle of weakness, people wreak havoc on themselves and those around them.

They injure the self-esteem of those around them and those people begin to stop loving themselves - retreating into their masks of behavior that offers only momentary self-fulfillment. It becomes a vicious cycle. You get screwed over and hurt so you do it to the next person in line until we are raising a generation of people who thrive on hiding in their masks. People who no longer know who they really are other than the sick twisted monster the world has created. We chew each other up and spit them back into the world, waiting for the next innocent victim to come along so they can be shown how the real world works... how nothing is sacred...nothing is safe.

Haven't you grown tired of this never ending merry-go-round? Then decide today. Who will you be? Will you let fear of being yourself in your purest form, glistening and glowing, rule your life? Will you let it hold you back from what you truly can be? Will you fall face down before it?

well, the choice is yours, as always.

Today I am throwing free the shackles of fear even knowing how bitterly I can be hurt. I am letting go of every injustice in my life and praying for forgiveness for those that I have done to others. I see this day before me the only real certainty I have ever known in my life.

I know what I want. I don't know how to get it, as of yet, but I know what I want and today, after removing every callous from my heart and letting go of every wound...I am ready to lay my heart on the line and say — Lord, do with it as You must because it is in Your hands. What should be the most terrifying moment in life actually brings relief because there is no looking back, just forward as I step into the new dawn of my life.

Sorry for rambling on..but, wow, I got started and I couldn't stop. When you know for certain what direction you want your life to go on, it's funny but it doesn't feel like I can stop...

I knew that the poem would be a treasure to her friends and so we loaded the trunk with the gift bags and headed up for the recital.

On arrival, we found our way inside Butler Church on the edge of campus. How many times had I been in this sanctuary for orientation and programs? A lot. As I sat there and gazed around, I realized that my heart, like a big, dumb dog, was bouncing around, waiting for Rebekah to appear from around a column and come sit beside me. Even as my mind scolded "don't be stupid, she is NOT here" my heart was not listening.

Instead, with every throb it seemed to be swiveling its neck and lolloping around, sure that Rebekah was near. So I discovered that your mind can know things that it takes the heart a lot longer to get a hold of. The mind can hold cold hard facts but the heart is still believing and searching for what it longs for.

Jimmy's recital was wonderful and it was great to see everyone. I handed out the little gift bags and got warm hugs from each of Rebekah's friends. Driving home, there was a sense of ripping or tearing as my heart began to KNOW that we could go to all of the familiar spots, see all the familiar faces, hear all of the familiar voices, and yet SHE would not appear. It was a collapse of the final suspension of numbness and pain flooded in.

Two weeks later, we had an appointment with those same wonderful students.

In 2003, when Rebekah and I had heard about the movie *The Passion of the Christ,* we had wondered if we could endure it. She smiled and said, "Here is what we will do. I will put my hand over your mouth and you can place yours over mine, and we will get through it."

Since she was not there to go with me, her friends came. There were a dozen of us who filed into the theater and watched the film together.

Caleb and Sam were on either side of me so I had my "guys" right there. There were portions of the film that hurt so bad, I thought that I would need a hand over my mouth. In the film, when Mary's hands just relaxed and let the stones that she had grasped fall to the ground, I knew the same powerless sensation of not being able to hold on. The film was a powerful and tender reminder to me. I am certainly not the first to suffer pain and loss.

Everyone came back over to our home afterwards for pizza and we had a chance to catch up on their lives and their laughter rang once again in our home.

Students from Fresno Pacific sharing their memories of Rebekah.

THE WHITE HOUSE

WASHINGTON

March 19, 2004

Ms. Rona Swanson
2420 North Bradley Street
Visalia, California 93292

Dear Ms. Swanson:

I am saddened to learn of the loss of your daughter, Rebekah.
I hope you will take comfort in the support of your family and
friends.

Laura and I send our heartfelt sympathy to you and your family.
You are in our thoughts and prayers during this difficult time.

Sincerely,

George W. Bush

Gone Gray

I sat in my office. I had cleared my calendar. I was sitting at my desk. It had been a couple of months since Rebekah's passing. I had done all of the things that I could think of to do;notifying Social Security, filing her life insurance claims, everything was done. Well, I was still waiting on the accident report but the officer had been very kind and promised she would mail a copy to me once completed. I had ordered the gravestone complete with lilacs and instead of describing Rebekah as beloved daughter and friend, I quoted her when we had listened to *I Can Only Imagine* and I had said, " I wonder what my response will be."

She had smiled and said, "Oh, Mom, I'm gonna dance!" and so I put that on her grave. It made me smile just thinking about it because we used to put a CD on the stereo and then one of us was the dancer while the other was the audience. We would have to put together an interpretive dance and we had so much fun being totally ridiculous with one another. Sometimes we would laugh until we cried, but, unlike me, Rebekah really was a very good dancer.

I received a lovely notice from our State Senator that in memoriam of Rebekah's life, the Senate had adjourned on February 17th. Then Sam brought me a package whose return address was the White House, Washington, DC. It said,

> I am saddened to learn of the loss of your daughter, Rebekah. I hope you will take comfort in the support of your family and friends.
>
> Laura and I send our heartfelt sympathy to you and your family. You are in our thoughts and prayers during this difficult time.
>
> Sincerely,
>
> George W. Bush

I wrote a thank you note back and told him that one of Rebekah's big goals for 2004 had been to cast her vote for his re-election. She had campaigned hard for him in 2000, even though she had not been old enough to vote. I told him that it was probably very bad theology, but if those who have gone ahead can organize angels to help out, he could count on her!

It was precious to me to receive such sweet communications and I was very grateful, but what I longed for was her.

I was reading through e-mails that we had sent back and forth when she was in England and came upon one written about a year before.

> Dear Mom,
>
>   I love you more than words would be able to explain. I hope that you know that. Your love and your willingness to love people and keep on giving every day without tiring astounds me. I am so very proud to call you my mother. No matter where I am or what I am doing, you will always be in my heart. We are bonded by blood, but even more than that by choice. You are the smile in my soul and the drive that keeps me going. Thank you for everything that you have been, everything that you are, and everything that you will be. Every piece of it, every moment is more than most people could hope to achieve in a lifetime. Yet every day you live with so much passion and love. I know that God is so very proud to call you His child and He has blessed me beyond measure by making you my mother.
>
> Eternally yours,
> Rebekah Marie Swanson

I sat and stared at that letter, tears streaming down my cheeks.

There is not a mother on the face of the earth who wouldn't love such a letter from her daughter. And that loving and delightful expression of love was not a rarity. It was the norm – daily, abundant, joyous communications that flowed into my every day moments. Now there were none. What had been a flood of warmth and vibrant life was cut off and the amputation of that source left me hemorrhaging away. As I surveyed my life I did not think I would even care if I bled on out.

Of course, I knew it was wrong for me to be that low, that resigned, that defeated, but I did not care.

I felt the whisper of God speak to my heart. "Her race is completed, but not yours!"

"God," I prayed. " All the world feels like it has gone gray for me. No color, no life, no joy. What am I supposed to do with that?" I laid my weary head onto my arms on my desktop, feeling overwhelmed.

As I was still, I felt a whisper in my soul. "Remember when you were a girl, in the winter, how all of the world would look colorless and gray. And you would sprinkle birdseed out on the snow? Remember what it was like when a cardinal would appear? How your heart would lift? I will send a cardinal to you each day. Not a literal one, but a messenger of color and beauty. But it will be like the little *Highlights* hidden pictures. You are going to have to open your eyes and LOOK for them!"

I sat up and prayed, "You have a deal! I will open my eyes, but you will have to send some sort of import of Joy because I am drowning here!"

That evening, on the way home, the sky was painted with crimsons and neon orange and hot pinks and purples — and there was a huge oak tree, its naked limbs lifted like hands to the kaleidoscope sky.

"Cardinal number one!" I shouted. "Found you!" and my drive home was not a strained sprint to seclusion but a gentle and intimate time with the God who sees and knows and loves us so much He meets us where we are and helps us rise again.

Doing Well?

Friends would remark about how well we were doing and Sam and I would laugh.Caleb had come to me a few weeks after Rebekah passed away and summed it up best, "Mom, if you were running the streets naked and insane, I would not be surprised because I know how much you love her, but I'm glad you're not because I could not have borne losing both of you at once."

I think pain is a strange distillery where God pours our tears to refine them into liquid diamonds because each one that slid down Caleb's cheek was like a gem to me. It was not that I liked seeing him sad, but rather that the shared intimacy of our grief comforted and soothed me deeply. There was a soft hush to my soul in Caleb's presence, but I learned that even that comfort could be mis-used and twisted into something unhealthy so I gently treasured those rare moments of shared sorrow and memory together. I felt warned in my soul not to make the sorrow a camping place, not to strike a banner, and set up residence there. I had seen people wrap such loss around them like a shroud and, even though tempting, I knew it would not be good for any of us.

I was functioning. Getting up every day and putting one foot in front of the other. Still, Sam and I had a half-joking solemn agreement that we would have to check one another before we left the house — just to make sure we did not forget our clothing!

Then a friend came to the office and begged me to promise I would not get on drugs.

I chuckled and said robotically, "I will not get on drugs!" But he chided, saying doctors will prescribe lots of stuff if you are depressed to which I replied in all seriousness, "I promise, I will not get on drugs, illegal or otherwise!"

Then a long-time family friend came and made us promise that we would seek counseling if our marriage was on the rocks. "Promise me you will not get divorced," he pleaded.

"We promise," we vowed, holding one another's hand, "we will not get divorced."

"You have to understand," Sam said, "I grabbed hold of one of God's legs and Rona grabbed the other and He has been carrying us ever since. We are not letting go!"

But we realized that people had seen the kind of wreckage that grief can bring and did not want to see us destroyed. And we knew that there was no hope to be healed of our shattered lives except through the Maker of Heaven and Earth. He alone had the skill to start putting all of the tiny shards of our broken hearts back together.

I knew that I could lose myself in grief if I wandered in too deep, drowning in the huge ocean of loss that stretched beyond the horizon, but also knew that I needed to be honest and deal with the reality of the wounding as well. I tried to write about the process.

———————

Some days the sky glowers down and I bow beneath the oppressive gloom
    Some days my knees buckle and fold
Some days the atmosphere seems too thin
    with not enough air to breathe
Some days I ache inside and the pain of her absence
    wracks my body without mercy
Some days I look around in bewilderment
    A stranger in a barren landscape
Some days there is no color, no joy
    And my ear hears only silence
Some days my skin feels like a parched field
    Suffering from the drought of her caresses
Some days my heart feels ancient and cold
    No nutrients of her extravagant love renewing and softening
Some days I find myself beside a sea of sorrow, slowly searching the horizon
    Hearing the waters lap at my feet
Some days I look to the waters, wondering how far I could move into them
    Before I would be engulfed in the depths of my grief
So...

Each day I will learn to walk gently beside these waters
    Each day I will look for a glimpse of light
Each day I will rejoice in a flash of color
    A lilting birdsong, a flower in bloom
Each day I will hum a new melody, in harmony with old treasured songs
    I will allow the waters to splash me and I will remember
Each day the pain will recede as I move with patience
    And I will discover that the replenishing well of love has not run dry
Each day I will find new outlets
    And discover rippling freshets in memory as well

Each day I will be reminded that the Source of all the joys,
 All the laughter and song and refreshment lives in
Each day...and when my numbered days are ended
 And I soar beyond this sea
Each day will dissolve into eternity and the teasing nibbles of joy here tasted
 Will be known complete in His presence as we gather at His feet

---

True to the bargain, the daily little cardinals were arriving; sometimes a card, a flower, a bird, an e-mail — but always, always, faithfully, a bright delight each day.

I tried to describe my quiet time, alone with God. There was not a human that could deal with all of my pain, my loss, my agony. But I found that I could pour out my heart before God and He would begin to resolve my severe trauma.

I have stumbled upon a rare place as I cry, blinded and wounded, cry for Jesus. In this desolate wilderness, gray and barren, a crevice opens. A vapor of sweet perfume rises and Jesus whispers but my concussed ears perceive no meaning.

"Broken, broken," I call.

He whispers again, but I can't catch the words.

"My heart is shattered," I moan.

Still He whispers and the sweetness rises.

"Ruin, cry ruin, utter ruin," my heart screams.

But I hear His words now. Gentle and calm, answering my despair.

Warm and fluid they rise to me... "Only love, only love, only love."

I close my eyes to listen as the words envelope and bathe my writhing spirit and dying heart.

"Only love, only love, only love"

I hear and in flashes of moments and meaning, brightness sears my eyes and lifts my heart.

"Yes, only love," I answer and take a faltering step.

"Only love," He sings, sending me on my way, yet lets me return again.

I sit beside the deep place. Mysteries live there.

His whispers rise like incense upon the perfumed air

I sit beside the deep place. I long to know Him more.

When all seemed lost and ruined, He opened wide this floor.

I sit beside the deep place. Still broken but much more.

Content in a Redeemer who lives forevermore.

Sometimes I wish that I could look into people's eyes and not worry anymore about what they think or how they feel because they hurt me and I should not care about them anymore.

Sometimes I wish that I could hear what people say, but not really listen, not let it become something that goes into me and festers like a disease that will eat away at me for the rest of my existence.

Sometimes I wish that I could be someone who was not hurt so easily by people, people that I love and trust (maybe they did not deserve either and that is why I am suffering now).

Sometimes I wish that I could be someone that I am not. I need to be hard so that no one can get to, no one can touch or hurt.

Sometimes I wish that I could take away all the past, all the memories and just wipe the slate clean to where I can start completely new.

Sometimes I wish that I could just be someone who no one knows anything about so they have no presumptions of me and I could just build anew.

Sometimes I wish that I could just have new friends, a new home, a new country, a new story that no one knows the end to.

Sometimes I wish that I could just be anyone but me.

Daniel

When we brought Rebekah's things home from college, there had been an un-mailed card to Marc and Lynda Unger's son, Daniel, who was in Iraq. I asked Marc if Daniel would still want me to send it, and Marc communicated with him via e-mail. Daniel had indeed wanted to receive it, so off it went.

We had started a support group for the local Guard unit after 9/11. Inspired by the book *Once Upon A Town* about a community – North Platte, Nebraska – where my parents live, and their determination to meet every train transporting troops during World War II with food and fun as they stopped for refueling there. Obviously, our little effort was on a much smaller scale. We held monthly meetings on Saturday afternoons at the armory and always had presents and birthday cake for the children celebrating birthdays.

I would entertain the children with games and activities so that their mothers would be able to socialize and talk frankly together. We organized special events at the holidays and got to know the families really well. Rebekah had been eager to participate if she was home for the weekend.

The first year, we organized a picnic for Memorial Day at Mooney Grove Park, a spacious green space interspersed with massive oak trees and winding water canals. I got a call from a family offering to provide music and that is how I came to know the Ungers. They arrived with a trailer full of instruments and Daniel, Marc the Dad, younger brother David, and another friend who was a classical guitarist, unloaded drums and guitars and keyboards and they began to play. Lynda and her daughters, Elizabeth and Anna, helped set up the tables and played with the children in attendance. Even though the event was in May, it grew warm as the afternoon wore on and Daniel was in the direct sun but he played cheerfully and did not pause to eat or drink until we were winding down the day.

The soldier's families took their tired but happy children home and the Ungers stayed behind, helping take down the bunting and patriotic tablecloths. I made sure that Daniel and the rest of the band got plenty to eat before we shut down the grill and stowed away the food. I had a chance to talk with Daniel for awhile as he sipped a cold soda. He had plans to enlist. Although he was a star baseball player on his high school team and had been offered scholarships, he felt that it was his duty, really a call on his life, to enlist. Before we departed, I asked if he would like a pen pal. "Really?" he had asked and I assured him I would be happy to write. And I did.

At the time of the Memorial Day picnic, Rebekah was still studying abroad in England, but when she came home she joined me in writing to Daniel. So it was that her last note was directed to him.

Once she was stateside again, she had one brief opportunity to meet Daniel as he and his unit were at the armory on the same Saturday that we were doing family support for deployed soldiers. When we had first started the effort, the families of the soldiers were not that concerned, even though their loved ones were being deployed to Iraq. After all, their job was not combat but support. They were going to be driving the convoys of supplies, so how tough could that be? It did not take us long to KNOW how tough that could be and the care-free meetings became times of prayer and support and huddled sanctuary.

But the day that Daniel's unit was at the armory the commander asked to speak to me in his office. It was our Christmas meeting. Daniel's family had come to provide music for the deployed soldier's families and take Daniel home for the holidays. We had back-packs and stuffed animals and treats for all of the children. It was a festive day. I joked with the commander as he led me away from the children's game I was leading, asking if I was in trouble. He shook his head no, but he was also grim-faced. Once inside his office, he introduced me to another officer in charge of Daniel's unit, and he explained that they had received deployment orders. His unit —Daniel's unit — was a combat unit, and the news of their deployment felt like a punch in the stomach.

He asked if I would be willing to help in family support for his unit as well.

"Yes," I said without hesitation, and then blurted out, "anything for Daniel."

The commander's face softened and he said he had heard great things about our connections and bonding among the families. "It can be difficult for Guard families because they are not housed on a base, they are not insulated from the public, they are truly citizen soldiers, so what you are doing in giving them a cohesive system to meet and connect is wonderful."

"It is truly my pleasure," I assured him.

"One more thing," he pleaded. "No one knows about these orders. These boys are just in from training and get to go and spend some time with family. Don't say anything about this to anyone."

I nodded, swallowing down the lump in my throat. As I walked from his office, I could see Rebekah. She had worn a red sweater as part of the holiday cheer and she was giving "airplane rides" to the children, holding them by their hands and twirling them in circles, their feet airborne as she spun. They had formed a line and once done, they would race to get back in line to ride on the Rebekah "plane". She was laughing and winded when I came over. I told the kids it was time for cake and we went and sang Happy Birthday to all of our birthday people and handed out the cake.

There was plenty left over and so we cut it up and served it out to the young men of Daniel's unit as they lounged out in the big armory bay. Looking into each of their eyes, I was praying for them, knowing they would soon face extreme challenges and deprivations.

That had been December. Rebekah and Daniel had had an opportunity to speak only briefly that day but they had corresponded via letters. Now Daniel had written several times from Iraq. He was a very faithful pen pal and wrote to me lovingly about how much Rebekah's letters had meant to him.

I wrote back.

Dear Daniel,
   You are in our prayers every single day, and we know that you are continually in the loving sight of our Lord and King. We have learned in a very deep way that we can trust Him in all things and that He is faithful...even when we are too weak to stand on our own He holds our hand and guides us on.

   We got a call this last week from the President of Fresno Pacific University. He said that Rebekah's professors had come to see him and had shown that even before this last semester, Rebekah had earned her degrees, and they very much wanted to present them to honor her work, even though it will have to be done posthumously. The president called to make sure that it would not disturb us to have that happen and to see if I would receive it on behalf of Rebekah. I told him I would be proud to.

The family of Rebekah Swanson was given a posthumous degree. Swanson, a senior English and psychology major from Visalia, was killed in an automobile accident during the school year. Billie Jean Wiebe (pictured), English faculty, and Phillip Collier, psychology faculty, presented the degree.

As I have been thinking of all of the honors and achievements that we can receive in our lifetimes, one thing is so very crystal clear. To know the Lord and to know His love for us is the greatest thing that any man or woman can accomplish. Secondly, to love all those who are seeking Him and to encourage them in any way that we can. I was reading about Jesus – a bruised reed, He will not break...a smoldering wick He will not snuff. He came to nurture the broken and bruised and to try and bring a flame to tiny sparks of desire for Him. I pray that God will teach me to be patient with those who are seeking him.

Much love,
Rona

❧ *Rebekah's Journal* ❧

Dear Daniel,

Hey there! My name is Rebekah Swanson. I'm Rona Swanson's daughter. My mom recently told me that she knew a very nice young man who was going through basic training right now and that you could probably use a pen pal. I know that when my brother, Caleb, was in boot camp, getting mail brought him loads of joy. So I thought that I would shoot a letter out your way.

It still impresses me today when I hear that more people are joining the ranks of our military. From my travels and interacting with different people all over the globe, I have been amazed by our generation and how far separated they have become from strong moral standing. It seems that today a large majority of people do things not based on what is right and honorable, but instead based on what is good for them at the time. I applaud you on your commitment to serving in the military and through that (most likely) sacrificing some monetary happiness for yourself, but doing what is best for God and country. It's commendable.

I can remember when Caleb was in boot camp, some (a lot of) days it was so hard for him to stay motivated and keep committed to the cause. This can be such a difficult task when there is no one around you to encourage you and motivate you. I'm glad to hear that you are still holding tight to the best motivator of all, God. Lately, I have been reading "The Road Less Traveled" by M. Scott Peck. He is such an amazing writer, but says things in such simple terms that anyone could understand. Here is a passage that I thought you might enjoy:

"Life is difficult. This is a great truth, one of the greatest truths. It is a great truth because once we truly see this truth, we transcend it. Once we truly know that life is difficult - once we truly understand and accept it - then life is no longer difficult. Because once it is accepted, the fact that life is difficult no longer matters. Most do not fully see this truth that life is difficult. Instead they moan more or less incessantly, noisily or subtly, about the enormity of their problems, their burdens, and their difficulties as if life were generally easy, as if life should be easy. They voice their belief - noisily or subtly - that their difficulties represent a unique kind of affliction that should not be and that has somehow been especially visited upon them, or else upon their families, their tribe, their class, their nation, their race or even their species, and not upon others. I know about this moaning because I have done my share."

(continued...)

I love that passage. I think that some days we can get so caught up in what is afflicting us that we do not see that the rest of the world is hurting. I know that I am guilty of this at many times. It can be hard to realize that your pain is not unique and that many have gone through it before you. It seems from your letter to my mom (which she shared with me) that you have already learned this in abundance and are happily going about your training. With a bright outlook and a happy attitude, you can do anything!

I hope that you are having a wonderful day filled with many blessings and bonding with the people around you.

Until later...

Rebekah's first letter to Daniel

Wedding Announcement

Caleb and Missy set the date for their wedding in May and asked me if I would go along with them as they traveled to Fresno and David's Bridal Shop. I was honored to be asked and sat in the back seat as we drove the 30 or so miles north. Part of the route took us directly past the tri-layered freeway exchange where Rebekah had left the upper tier, hit half-way down, and then fallen all of the rest of the way to the ground below. We had been chatting and listening to music but it grew quiet as we neared the spot. It was as if we all stopped breathing. Caleb reached back between the seats to grab hold of my hand and we squeezed each others' fingers as we looked into one another's eyes. Of course, Caleb had never (and will never) know childbirth but as we passed the place where his baby sis had lost her life...my beating heart was going through a contraction so severe that if I had had a coach, they would have had to remind me to keep breathing. Missy was driving, which was a good thing because Caleb and I were a temporary mess but as the miles ticked away and we were able to tune in on the music and the events about to occur, we gained our composure back. They had a Swithfoot CD playing and I kept playing over and over "This is your life...are you who you want to be? Don't close your eyes... don't close your eyes". The words were a profound reminder to keep on living...even when you feel like dying.

The shop was lovely. I wandered through row upon row upon row of beautiful gowns. Missy's parents were there as well and explored light-heartedly. I, on the other hand, had to keep reining my emotions in. As my fingertips ran across the lace and satin and intricate embroidery, my heart kept reminding me that I would never be able to select Rebekah's gown, never sit and try and hold back tears as she radiantly

The Marriage Ceremony Uniting

Melissa Ann Kirksey
&
Caleb Michael Swanson

May 28, 2004

Parents of the Bride
Mr. & Mrs. Steve Kirksey

Parents of the Groom
Mr. & Mrs. Samuel & Rona Temaino
(Swanson)

Maid of Honor
Jennifer Stevens

Brides Maid
Melisa Prins

Best Man
Brian Merson

Groomsman
Jeremy Denham

Flower Girl
Anamarie Bloxe

Pastor
Dennis Doane

String Quartet
Molly Havard - Violin
Jessica Hong - Violin
Karli Leal - Viola
Heather Bryan - Cello

Thank you for blessing our special day

took her vows, never! I had to hush those whispers of loss and focus on the joy of my soon-to-be daughter-in-law and their eager preparation for the wedding day. I lingered right outside the dressing room and helped Missy up onto the high stand with each and every new fitting. Caleb was not anywhere near, promising to see his bride only on her wedding day, but I would sometimes need to go and locate Missy's parents because there were so many other things in the store to look at than just gowns.

A selection was made, the arrangements made for her final fitting and all of the items needed for the outfitting of the bride. Sara, Caleb's big sister, had agreed to help with decorations and the flowers and Missy was highly organized in making sure everything was accomplished in plenty of time to have announcements and invitations and facilities. Everything was set.

∞ *Rebekah's Journal* ∞

Have you ever noticed that the worst way to miss someone is when they are right beside you and yet you can never have them...when the moment you can't feel them under your fingertips you miss them? Have you ever wondered which hurts the most: saying something and wishing you had not, or saying nothing and wishing you had?

I guess the most important things are the hardest things to say...They are the things you get ashamed of because words diminish them; words shrink things that seemed timeless when they were in your head...to no more than living size when they are brought out...Don't be afraid to tell someone you love them. If you do, they might break your heart... but if you don't, you might break theirs. Have you ever decided not to become a couple because you were so afraid of losing what you already had with that person?

Your heart decides who it likes and who it doesn't. You can't tell your heart what to do. It does it on its own when you least suspect it, or even when you don't want it to. Have you ever wanted to love someone with everything you had, but that other person was too afraid to let you? Too many of us stay closed up because we are too afraid to care too much...for fear that the other person does not care as much, or at all.

Have you ever loved someone and they had absolutely no idea what so ever? or fell for your best friend in the entire world, and then sat around and watched them fall for someone else? Have you ever denied your feelings for someone because your fear of rejection was too hard to handle? we tell lies when we are afraid...afraid of what we don't know, afraid of what others will think, afraid of what will be found out about us. But every time we tell a lie...the thing we fear grows stronger. Life is all about risks and it requires you to jump.

Don't be a person who has to look back and wonder what they would have, or could have had. No one waits forever...

Easter

My birthday was Palm Sunday and then Easter. Easter...with flowers starting to bloom and days warming and growing longer...Easter. I found a poem of Rebekah's and printed it on pretty paper and put it in frames for Caleb and Sara when they came over for our shared meal.

☙ *Rebekah's Journal* ☙

Price

wretched and broken,
I come before you
having nothing to offer,
but my tainted heart.
It is not a worthy gift
for the king of all kings,
but it is what I have for you.
will it be enough?
I crawl before you
too weak to walk.
In awe of the greatness before me,
not able to look into Your face.
Timidly I kneel and then lay before you
submitting all of me to you.
Broken and wretched, though I am,
I am all yours.
My heart weeps
for all I have done wrong.

My submission before you
is not enough to repay the debts I owe.
Yet, You, full of perfection,
have paid them all in full for me
with the sacrifice of Your son
upon a solitary tree.

———————

I can rejoice that death – ugly death – you do not get the final word here. Thank you God, for the hope of Resurrection!

∽ *Rebekah's Journal* ∽

My favorite holiday is Easter. It's my favorite holiday because my father never calls on Easter. I also love it because of what it represents – our rebirth and growth. How much God gave up for us, but that it wasn't all for vain. Great holiday.

TRAFFIC COLLISION REPORT

STATE OF CALIFORNIA
CHP 555 CARS Page 1 (Rev 1-03) OPI 061

JUDICIAL DISTRICT			LOCAL REPORT NUMBER
FRESNO SUPERIOR	BEAT 410		2004-01-0133

	NUMBER INJURED 0	HIT & RUN FELONY	CITY # FRESNO	REPORTING DISTRICT					NCIC # 9435	OFFICER I.D. 15666

SPECIAL CONDITIONS
FATAL

NUMBER KILLED 1	HIT & RUN MISDEMEANOR	COUNTY FRESNO	MO DAY YEAR 1/13/2004	TIME (2400) 2343	PHOTOGRAPHS BY: OFC KRAMER

		DAY OF WEEK TUESDAY	TOW AWAY [X] YES [ ] NO	OFC LYNN

	STATE HWY REL [X] YES [ ] NO	OFC BANTA

LOCATION

COLLISION OCCURRED ON:
SR-41 SB TRANSITION ROAD TO SR-180 E/B

LICENSE NUMBER
3DER127

MILEPOST INFORMATION:

	VEH. YEAR 1993	MAKE / MODEL / COLOR FORD ESCORT WHI

AT INTERSECTION WITH:
[X] OR 791 FEET SOUTH OF OLIVE AVENUE U/C

STATE CA	CLASS C	AIR BAG P	SAFETY EQUIP. K/C	OWNER'S NAME [X] SAME AS DRIVER

PARTY 1

DRIVER'S LICENSE NUMBER
B9133085

OWNER'S ADDRESS [X] SAME AS DRIVER

DRIVER [X]

NAME (FIRST, MIDDLE, LAST)
REBEKAH MARIE SWANSON

[X] OFFICER	[ ] DRIVER

DISPOSITION OF VEHICLE ON ORDERS OF:
ROMO'S TOW - (559)275-4823 [X] NONE APP

PEDESTRIAN

STREET ADDRESS

CA

PRIOR MECH. DEFECTS

PARKED VEHICLE

CITY / STATE / ZIP VISALIA			WEIGHT	BIRTHDATE Mo Day 11/19/1982 Year	RACE W	VEHICLE IDENTIFICATION NUMBER	DESCRIBE VEHICLE DAMAGE [ ] NONE [ ] MINOR [ ] ROLLOVER

BICYCLIST

SEX F	HAIR BRN	EYES BLU	HEIGHT 5-07		BUSINESS PHONE	VEHICLE TYPE 01	[ ] UNK [X] MAJOR [ ] MOD

		CA			DOT	MC/MX

OTHER

HOME PHONE

POLICY NUMBER

CAL-T	TCP/P/SC

INSURANCE CARRIER
PACIFIC PROPERTY

SPEED LIMIT 65	VEH. YEAR	MAKE / MODEL / COLOR

DIR OF TRAVEL ON STREET OR HIGHWAY

		STATE	CLASS	AIR BAG	SAFETY EQUIP		SAME AS DRIVER

OWNER'S NAME

39

Accident Report

A woman had been assigned to investigate Rebekah's accident, and she had stayed in touch with me. I asked if I could have a copy of the completed report. She had promised she would get it to me.

It arrived on April 21st, and even though I had requested it, there was a part of me that cringed when I saw it. I waited until Sam had gone to worship band rehearsal before I opened it. It was a thick group of papers stapled together, and I saw *Page 1 of 17* on the cover page. Seventeen pages!

I took a deep, raggedy breath and started reading. I had read accident reports before. I am an insurance agent — but it did not matter because this report described the last moments of my baby girl's life. I began reading about witnesses. I did not know there were witnesses. I wanted to get a phone and call them, ask them to tell me *everything*, but I read on. The officer had told me that the last two pages had black and white photos, taken at the scene a day or two later and of the car at the towing yard. There would be no photos of Rebekah at the scene but nevertheless, as I turned each successive page my heart was pounding in my chest. I came to the end and the black and white photos of her crumpled, mangled car and the scrapes and gouges of concrete and metal shards and scraps.

Astoundingly, her car had left an upper tier of freeway, fallen to a mid-level freeway and impacted there, breaking in two. The engine fell one way and the rest of the car, with Rebekah still inside, fell the other way. Her car landed on its tires, headed the right way on the bottom freeway shoulder and no one else was harmed, even though there were cars passing by.

I sat with my head bowed. I had made it to the end of the report. My heart had not exploded and I was still breathing. I was impressed. I slid the report back into the envelope. I knew I would need to look at it again because my mind was spinning and completely unable to take anything further in.

I turned on the shower and let the hot water sting on my skin. The report had overwhelmed me with the sheer height and impact of what had occurred. I felt a physical need to DO SOMETHING! The adrenaline surge stung to my very marrow. And yet even as I wanted to apply all of my might to run, and warn, and prevent, I knew that there was nothing that I could do to change the stark facts on that report or the result of the events that occurred. Rebekah's car had left the freeway. For the brief period before the first impact, she had to know what was happening. A witness talked about her brake lights flashing. She had to know, and it hurt to think of any panic, any fear, that might have gripped her heart for even a brief time.

I leaned in under the stinging spray of the shower, letting it pour on my head and shoulders, my hands braced against the wall, my eyes squeezed shut, overcome with pain.

Then I felt a whisper to my heart, as if God were leaning over my shoulder. "You have seen the physical report. Would you like to see mine?"

In that darkness of eyes closed tight, a little movie began running in my mind. I could see Rebekah's car approaching the on-ramp and begin its ascent. I watched, almost as if I were poised in mid-air above the freeway. As her car was rising, suddenly around me the air lit up with row upon row upon row of angels. It was like stadium seating at a bowl game and they were focused on Rebekah's car as it began to leave the upper tier and fly airborne. As her car crashed into the first level of lower freeway, I saw an angel standing beside her car and he held out his hand, lifting Rebekah from the shattering, smashing, descending wreckage like a princess from her carriage. The look on Rebekah's face was one of joy and surprise. She was whole, complete, and glowing with light. Then suddenly, Rebekah and all of the angels lifted up and away.

I stood under the shower and let the water blend with my tears. I thought of the scripture, "Eye has not seen or ear heard the glory that awaits us" and wondered once again what mysteries await. Our bodies aren't eternal but we sure are meant for something more than this!

∽ *Rebekah's Journal* ∽

During my junior year in high school I was accepted to be in the Celebrants Singers, a professional Christian choir and orchestra. I was set to tour with the summer Celebrants as the first chair flautist on the Central American team.

As Celebrant Singers is a non-profit organization, all team members are required to raise half of the money needed to train and send members on their missionary trip. With less than two months to go before I left for music camp, I had to raise almost $4,000 in missionary support. I began the task of raising money by writing a letter about this opportunity and sending it to almost everyone that I know.

The initial response was remarkable, and I thought I would soon be on my way to having it done. In the midst of all of the activity, my mother was contacted to host a table for one of our state senators. It was a $150 a plate dinner. If you knew my mom, you would know that she does not take commitments lightly and envisioned herself writing a check for ten tickets if she agreed. She called Senator Poochigian's wife, Debbie, to tell her that she would be unable to sponsor an entire table because of the financial commitment to me.

Debbie was excited to hear about my opportunity and asked my mom if I could find a few singers to come and perform at the dinner with me. After contacting the Celebrant Singers office, my mom found out that the night of the dinner all of the full-time Celebrants would be at music camp, and that no one would be able to come and sing with me. My mom was about to call Debbie and tell her that I would not be able to perform at the dinner. Before she declined the invitation, I offered to perform by myself.

"Really?" my mom replied, her voice laced in skepticism.

(continued...)

I pulled out my flute and played the National Anthem for her. "See," I said with confidence, "no big deal."

My mom called Debbie back and told her that I would be glad to play the National Anthem, but that I had been unable to find any vocalists.

Debbie was so excited and said that a flute solo would be just wonderful. For the next week, I practiced the National Anthem every night in preparation for my big performance.

Finally the big night arrived. I entered the Fresno Convention Center, my flute case on my shoulder and my mother by my side to see two thousand people swarming around the room. I felt my stomach drop to the floor and my heart begin to race. When I had told my mom that I would play at the dinner, I had imagined a couple hundred people at most, not two thousand! I began to have doubts about the performance and felt that I could barely remember my name — let alone the National Anthem!

My mom and I walked around the room and she stopped and talked to friends and acquaintances while I plotted how to get out of this. My mom decided that we should talk to Chuck and Debbie Poochigian, just to let them know that their flautist had arrived.

I checked out the band in the corner, wondering if the flute player there would like a nice patriotic solo. After all, who was I to steal the spotlight?

As mom talked to Chuck and Debbie, I gazed around about me, wondering how on earth I would be able to play with all of these people staring at me.

Debbie realized that I was nervous and tried to calm me down by telling me that most of the people attending were Armenian and not tremendously musical and that they would be thrilled if I just made a sound on my instrument. I began to calm down a bit. We were asked to take our seats and when we reached our table, I began to assemble my flute. Soon I was talking with a friend of the family and getting coached on how to not get nervous while performing when my name was called to come up on stage. I walked up on the platform and stood talking with other participants while I waited for my turn to perform.

After the flag salute I walked to center stage and looked over at my mom to try and calm my nerves. I then took a deep breath and played the National Anthem as the audience quietly sang along.

I had been so scared while I was performing but all of the people at our table said that it did not show at all. As we were getting ready to leave that night, many people congratulated me and remarked how amazing it was that I had not been nervous. (Shows what they know!!!!!)

The lessons I learned that night will stay with me for my whole life. I learned that while we may experience fear (or even terror!) regarding a challenge or a perceived threat, we need not be neutralized in our ability to respond. I trust that lesson will serve me well as I tour this summer, because you can believe that I am no longer intimidated raising my financial support.

(Rebekah's personal statement to the Celebrant Singers organization).

Pinning Ceremony

Caleb had graduated from the police academy in August 2003 but it was a long, slow process of interview and job applications. He was interested in going to work in northern California or even Washington or Oregon but he had been offered a position with our local Tulare County Sheriff's Department and so we gathered on Monday, May 3, 2004 for the pinning ceremony.

While we were seated and waiting for the dignitaries to arrive, I thought back over the previous August. I tried to think of something that would be unique and wonderful to do when Caleb graduated from the academy. Rebekah was just back from studying in England and so I came up with the idea that we would go for a horseback adventure up in the high Sierras. The kids had grown up with horses and we had left them behind when we moved down from the mountains so I knew they would love the chance to saddle up for a day. When Sam got wind of it, he got his feelings hurt at not being included, so I conferred with Caleb and Rebekah and he got invited too...with the stern warning that he better not wimp out on us (since he had zero horse experience!).

Early in the morning on August 9th, 2003, we arrived up above Shaver Lake nestled in the Sierra Nevada mountains. We had a guide named Brian and they put me right behind him on a pretty paint horse named KC. Then came Sam on a bay horse that they thought was named Reno (although by the end of the day Sam was calling him Larry after his best friend). Caleb came next and he was put on a MULE named Ruby. He was a bit put out...I mean, after all, he was the reason we were having this outing, he was the man of the hour, and it was supposed to be HORSE back riding but after a bit of a complaint, he climbed aboard. Rebekah brought up the rear on a pretty buckskin mare named Darcy. We began winding our way up switch-backing dirt trails sprinkled with pine needles and wildflowers. We stopped and took pictures after about an hour. We were a laughing and celebrating bunch and chatted gaily as we climbed higher and higher.

We lunched on sandwiches that I had packed as we sat on the ceiling of the Sierras, gazing down over blue lakes dotted in the valleys below us. We could see the tops of El Capitan and what would be Yosemite Valley.

Our guide said, "Well, you wanted today to be memorable, right?" We all nodded as the fresh, cool air played on our faces. We were taking it all in.

But Brian had further delights in mind. "We are going over Kaiser Pass!" he announced.

We went back to our mounts and climbed aboard. Brian began leading us up a rocky incline. The horses were following docilely but Ruby, Caleb's mule, stood looking at where we were headed and began flapping her ears.

Brian stopped and looked back.

"Kick her up," he hollered, and we could see Ruby's sides moving in and out like a bellows as Caleb squeezed his legs and kicked her belly. She looked determined to stand her ground.

"Herd her on up here," Brian hollered to Rebekah and she went into her cattle herding mode on Darcy, the buckskin mare, bumping right up against Ruby's bottom to get her moving.

It worked. Ruby joined us, none too happily, and we began a scramble up over loose shale and through rugged, rocky trails that proved how athletic our horses were. I had never taken a horse over the kind of rough terrain that we were passing through and wondered how Sam would do. We were on narrow ledges and leaping across ravines but he just kept his horse's nose behind mine, talking calmly to him as we went. Looking at him, I realized that sometimes ignorance IS bliss because this was a TRAIL RIDE for sure!

We got to the crest and dropped down to a sapphire blue lake where we let the horses have a blow and a nice drink. Knee-high, lush green grass rimmed the lake and then we rode into a wooded area that opened into an alpine meadow strewn with wild flowers of every hue. We got off and walked around for a bit to rest our legs and then it was time to head back down.

I was feeling a bit anxious because climbing up a steep incline with tricky footing is hard enough. Picking your way down can really be a challenge. I showed Sam how to brace his feet in the stirrups and lean back to help his horse keep balance. I was so busy watching him, I did not see that KC was taking a bit of a shortcut, leaping a ravine instead of tiptoeing down it. We went airborne and it was lucky I had my knees tucked tight. When Sam's horse followed suit, he acted like it was something he did everyday and even let out a whoop of joy.

As we came down the mountain and entered back into the tree line and wooded trail, Sam was talking about the *Man from Snowy River*. Brian waited until we got to a clearing and told Sam he could do his Snowy River routine. Off Sam went, careening down the steep hillside. I was holding my breath as he whooped and hollered and made it to the level path and waited for us to join him. Caleb and Rebekah were laughing, once they knew he was not going to break his neck, and we soon came to the corrals and unsaddled our horses and headed down the mountain.

We stopped for dinner at Brooks Ranch, a homestyle café. When we were walking in, I patted my jeans and dust flew out in clouds. "Taking a bit of the trail with you, pard?" Sam asked and we all realized what a dusty bunch we were. Tired and a bit stiff, we toasted one another with big glasses of iced tea. "And here's to Ruby," Caleb added, who had ended up being the nicest ride of all with her sturdy little hooves taking every challenge in stride. We had conquered Kaiser Pass. Rebekah wanted to get a tee-shirt to proudly wear. That day was a glistening, joyous day of sunlight and laughter.

The next day, Caleb, Rebekah, and I were in sun-burned misery, not realizing how thin the air was and how much exposure we received. The only person who came through the ride unscathed was Sam, the greenhorn. His Italian heritage and olive skin repelled the sunburn that we were dosing with Noxema and Solarcaine. We had

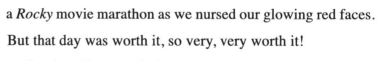

a *Rocky* movie marathon as we nursed our glowing red faces. But that day was worth it, so very, very worth it!

It echoed in my mind as we waited for the pinning ceremony to begin. Caleb had said that I would have the honors, but sitting next to Missy, his soon-to-be bride, I whispered, "This should be your place, not mine!"

She shook her head and leaned over to me. "You are his Mom," she said.

"I know," I countered, "but you will be his wife!"

But she would not hear of taking my place and so I proudly rose and put Caleb's pin on his uniform when they called for me, forever grateful for the generosity of the woman my son chose to be his bride.

⚭ *Rebekah's Journal* ⚭

Our guide knew that we wanted a real ride, so he took us on a real ride. He took us over Kaiser Pass. At first, Ruby refused to go up the pass. The look on her face was classic, like she was telling Brian, "There is no way in hell I am going up there." After we'd ridden it, we found out that barely anyone ever rides over that pass. I can see why. It is very steep and scary at spots. It was such a fabulous ride! Even with the way down in which Ruby and Darcy insisted on trotting downhill, which does wonders to your legs. I will never forget all the laughing and all the jokes with my brother. I will always remember our wonderful steeds.

When I was nine, I was baptized. That is still an amazingly precious day to me. On that day, not only was I baptized, but my brother was baptized. We were baptized together.

It is so precious to me still to this day. My brother and I grew in everything together, including our commitment to God. Sometimes I feel like I have gone so far from God and that I need to reinforce that I love Him. I know that He doesn't need to hear this, but I feel like He does. Maybe it's because I am someone who needs to be so constantly reminded that they are loved and needed that I think God is the same way.

I Love You, Mum

Of all the people
in my life
you've always been the one,
who's shown an
extra-special interest
in the things that I have done.

You've been there
to congratulate
and to commiserate as well,
you've been the one
who's picked me up
every time I fell...

Mother's Day

Caleb and Sara tried so hard to make Mother's Day wonderful for me. I had to laugh because Sara bought me cards that were the size of posters! Caleb bought me a tender Willow Tree figurine of Mother and Son to join the one of Mother and Daughter that my sister had sent to me. It was adorable and we all had dinner together before they headed home.

As the day wound down, I read a portion of Rebekah's journal from the year before:

∽ *Rebekah's Journal* ∽

It's Mother's Day in England on Sunday. So weird for me. Once again, the thought of making someone smile (my mother) took control of my actions and I bought her a very special Mother's Day card. A card that says "Mum" about seven times. She'll love it.

Walking back from Bath Road, I looked all around me. As I passed St. Philip and St. James parish I suddenly saw a clock in my head. The days are ticking of my time here. Soon I will no longer walk by the parish every day in this place that I have come to call home. Soon I will not choose between sweet and salted popcorn at the movie theater. Soon this will all be just a dream, a longing that will never die.

Four summers ago (I swear it wasn't that long ago), all that it took to make me happy was a cola champagne and walking down a dirt road with a pudgy little hand held in mine. El Salvador was my home for a short time, and it still owns a part of me. It took possession of the piece of me by giving me: sticky, grubby kisses from children who love more than you can imagine, the secret that money means nothing and people's smiles and joys hold so much more worth, and from the million other things that it taught me.

I want to be stuck in the continuum here where life and living are all that matter. No grades, no money, no politics, no war. All you need is love.

———————

I pulled out the card that had arrived from England the year before. She was right. It had Mum on it again and again, but it was her hand-written note that I read:

Happy Mother's Day, Mom!

I hope that you have an absolutely amazing day. I am sorry that I cannot be there with you for it, but know you are in my thoughts and prayers on this day that people around the United States celebrate mothers. You are also in my thoughts EVERY day.

Even though there is a physical distance between us, there is such a strong bond between us that will never be broken. Not only of blood, but also a bond of our spirit. You mean so very much to me, Mom.

I hope that you know this above all else. I know that I will be back soon and I am looking forward to catching up with you.

Have an amazing day, Mom. Enjoy it to the fullest. Sending lots of love on the American Mother's Day, all of the way from England!

Bekah

I stared at the words...physical distance, strong bond that will never be broken.

It is true. I feel it even now.

I love you...more than can be measured.

But my words echo back to me...and I miss her.

Sara is so kind. She longs to make it all better. She has even offered to come over and watch Jane Austen movies with me...but I smile and tell her I love her, HER, and always have. She cannot take the place of her little sister because then who would take her place?

But it is hard, trying to rise to the same level of joy and celebration when a part of your heart is screaming still.

Media Contact

Sam's youngest daughter, Kristen, flew in for Caleb's wedding. It is wonderful to have her with us. We went to dinner and had a chance to hear all about her life in Georgia.

Sam's birthday is May 25th (three days before the wedding) and having the rare privilege of seeing Kristen's face that day was the best present he could have had.

At my office the next day, I got a phone call from a local network affiliate news crew. "I need the contact information for a soldier's family," they said.

I had become pretty savvy about giving out information. I had been briefed after 9/11 that some of the terror threats had discussed terrorizing National Guard families. Since they were not in a protected base environment, I was urged to be even more protective of their identity and status.

"What information are you looking for?" I asked.

"We got word of a soldier killed in action in Iraq and want to reach the family," the female reporter replied. "He is from Exeter."

"Not Daniel Unger," I pleaded before I could even think.

"Yes," she replied.

I felt my stomach turn and my mind begin to reel. "Oh please," I begged. "Let the family have a little time to process this loss in private."

"We were going to use the story to tie in with Memorial Day," she explained.

"Don't send a news crew out to video their agony so publicly," I asked. " If you must have something on camera, come here. I have a friend who served in Viet Nam and we both know and love the entire Unger family so we can talk to you about Daniel as well."

The reporter agreed and so I called my friend Bill and he agreed to meet at my office after lunch. I went home and had lunch with Kristen, then headed back to the office and met Bill and the news crew there. We both shared about Daniel's selfless love of others and his burning desire to serve his country. We expressed our extreme love of the family and our grief at his loss.

After the news crew left, I had a good cry. Once I was composed, I called Marc and Lynda, just to tell them that I loved them and was praying for them. Between sobs, they thanked me. I knew all too well the breathless, ragged crying that they had undergone and that would sweep over them again and again in the days to come.

I promised to stay in touch and then got ready to go to the wedding rehearsal that evening. I did not mention anything to Caleb and Missy. Their heads were full of wedding and arrangements and making sure all went smooth. I wanted to assist in whatever way that I could.

The rehearsal went well and we had dinner together afterwards, full of laughter and love. Caleb got a chance to visit with Kristen, who he had nicknamed "Ankle-biter" from their younger years. She loved to have him call her that and thoroughly enjoyed the chance to spend some time with him.

Family was coming in for the wedding and there were so many things to remember and do that I was so glad to have Kristen around. Her boundless energy and willingness to go, go, go helped me so much.

∞ *Rebekah's Journal* ∞

Things that are new in my life:

* I have lost 1 stone in the last two weeks.

* I bought a '93 Ford Escort.

* I have no clue what I am going to do when I graduate.

* I am observing a high school poetry class.

* I am becoming a nun.

Memory: Growing up I measured my wealth in miniscule ways, ways that if people knew about them, they would laugh. When I was seven, we moved to Visalia. It was such a HUGE city (that is in comparison to Glennville – population 100). I was the little country mountain girl who never really watched TV and whose swimming pool was a scum-infested pond. Now we were in the big city where we had five channels on our television without cable and a community swimming pool that everyone in our neighborhood could use. We were RICH beyond measure. I thought that I had died and was in paradise. Then I met the other kids my age. They had loads of clothes and all of the newest toys. At christmas, they got toy after toy. I got sensible socks and jeans. I wasn't rich in their eyes. The years progressed, and I still always had the sensible things. Growing up, I never knew what GAP was.

In junior high, my best friend became obsessed with Bath and Body works products. They were all the craze. Everyone had Bath and Body works...everyone, that is, but me.

That year for my birthday I got $15. I contemplated what I would buy with it (or what I would save for, as was often the case) for a long time. Finally, I made my decision. I walked into Bath and Body works timidly and bought a medium size bottle of Country Apple lotion. I spent $14 on one bottle of lotion, almost all of my birthday money. This lotion was now my wealth, my richness, my ability to fit in. when friends were over, I would put it on to prove that I too was part of the Bath and Body works crowd.

I would offer it to them, secretly hoping they would refuse, but they would say yes and slather it on. when I would partake of my wealth, it would be in timid droplets, not wanting to squander it all at once or have it run dry too soon. when they would use it, it was treated like a never-ending supply...probably because theirs was! They didn't realize

(continued...)

it, but with every drop they took of my lotion, they were taking a drop of my self-worth. A piece of my ability to fit in. It all weighed on the balance of that medium-sized bottle having any liquid in it. When I was a sophomore in high school, my step-father had a heart attack. That night my mom bought Carl's Jr hamburgers for us (we hardly ever eat out) and went to the store and bought Clairol Herbal Essence shampoo (I'd never used anything but Suave).

Herbal Essence was now my wealth. I hoarded it and only used it on special occasions when I knew people would notice.

Whenever I lost something (in this case my security in human mortality) my mother would try to give me something back to restore my inner strength and put me at peace with myself and my surroundings once again. Funny how just a bottle of shampoo and conditioner could do that for me.

I hoarded those bottles of Herbal Essence more than I had hoarded anything else in my life. My sister always bothered me about it. She always harassed me about why I wouldn't let her use it. She could never understand that I felt rich and safe when I had something left in those bottles. It was like the woman with the never-ending jars of oil and cornmeal. She KNEW she would be okay if she still had the jars. I knew I would be okay if I had my Herbal Essence.

Now I am much older and life is not as simple. I buy Herbal Essence in the Costco size containers. I get a thrill every time I use it and still feel rich because I know what it means to me. People did not understand it then, and they don't understand what it means to me now.

My family has never been rich, but we have always had enough to sustain us. We have never had to go without, although we have been limited at times. I hold on to the small things in my life to remind me how rich I am. My HUGE bottles of Herbal Essence always remind me of the jubilance on my mother's face when she buys it for me because she can give me something ritzy that I absolutely love. She gets such joy out of knowing that I get to use my favorite shampoo every time I shower.

That is what makes it special.

That is what makes me rich.

It is not the price tag on the shampoo (I know it is really not that expensive in the scheme of things). It's not the labels on the clothes. It is the thought, the memory that each item induces that gives them worth.

Wedding Day

Blue sky and warm sunny day. We arrived at the wedding and there were so many beloved faces gathered around. There was the usual flurry of getting everyone where they needed to be, all dressed in their best and making sure all of the details were in place.

Missy's mom, Barb, and I were to light the candles. Both of our long lighters blew out as we began climbing the stairs. Barb said, "Let's just fake it!" and so we went through the motions and returned to our seats but the ushers re-lit our torches and brought them to us for a 2nd try. Laughing all of the way, we actually accomplished the task and found our seats again.

The ceremony was so lovely with a string quartet and Missy was absolutely radiant. Caleb's best man was Brian, a fellow Marine who now lived in Chicago. He had flown out to be by Caleb's side and he behaved impeccably.

After the wedding, we moved to a social hall across town where the meal and reception would be served. Missy's mother had lovingly prepared the food herself. We chatted with all of the guests while we waited for the wedding party to arrive. They were getting the photos done and so they were delayed a bit but it was nice to catch up with people we had not seen in some time.

Caleb and Missy arrived and the celebration was underway. The DJ made some announcements and the song from the movie Titanic – *My Heart Will Go On* – began playing as he mentioned that Caleb and Missie were so sorry that Rebekah was not present to share in their joy. The song did not play long, which was good, because it could sweep me away to seeing Rebekah, shiny-eyed, doing a perfect lip sync along with Celine, perfected with the dramatic fist to her heart as she sang along.

There was the father/daughter dance and then the mother/son dance. I am not really familiar with this tradition but Caleb was motioning me to join him so I stood and walked out on to the floor. As I came to him I asked, "You're not going to kill me with a song, are you?"

He leaned back and looked into my eyes and said, "I have never heard this song in my life, but it is nice so I chose it!"

I smiled as I wrapped an arm around him. "Well," I sighed. "that means we can have a nice visit, then." And we did, chatting about his week, my hopes that Brian would not let loose and make me want to run from the room if he got too rowdy, their honeymoon plans, and our need to collect all of the presents and take them to our home until their return. It was a very sweet and tender time.

Then came time for the toast. I was holding my breath when Brian rose. He was a gung-ho, testosterone king and I wondered what in the world he might say. But he looked at Caleb and said, "When we met in the Marine Corps, I thought this guy is soft, because you have such a kind heart. But I learned that you were my brother through and through, and I am so glad that I know you. Caleb, no matter where I am in the world, if you ever call and need me, I will be there. You will be my friend forever, and I am so proud to be your best man."

The room broke open with applause and I was able to gently observe people who were so dear congratulating Caleb and Missy. Caleb lifted Kristen up and spun her around when the music let loose and she was absolutely delighted with the big brother twirl.

Sara had put together silk and real flowers and every table was beautifully decorated. She beamed at her little brother as he came over to hug her tight.

We waited until the last person was gone after mealtime and cake cutting and Caleb and Missy were heading off to their honeymoon. We loaded all of the gifts and cards in our vehicle and headed on home.

To My Future Husband

You were all that was on my mind today.

It is crazy how it works.

No matter what I was doing

you somehow became the focus of my thoughts.

People came in and out of my life today.

I kept wondering if one of them was you.

How strange would that be?

To be in the same room with you a million times

but never realizing that you were the love of my life,

the man I have always been waiting for.

Two men asked me out today.

I do not think that either of them are you, but I am not sure.

I am so afraid of missing you because I'm not paying attention.

I am so scared that somehow my attention will be diverted
and I will miss you.

oh, sweet life, this could not happen.

I will know you when I see you.

From the sparkle in your eyes...to your open smile.

Until we meet...my dreams of you will have to be enough.

Boys

They think that they will
but they probably won't.
They think they do
but they might not.
It's all so clear
but it makes no sense.
They spend their whole life
attempting to get past this pretense.
They have a mind,
but no logic inside.
They have a heart
but forget where it resides.
They play the game
but they don't play fair.
They know it all
but does it get them anywhere?
They have all the tools
at their beck and call.
I've seen so many boys
is there a man among them all?

Guys

Boys in men's clothing
going through the day.
Trying to figure out
how to find their way.

Longing to be gentlemen,
knowing not what for.
Being courteous to girls,
even opening car doors.

Combing through their hair,
tucking in their shirts.
sticking to one girl,
instead of being flirts.

Learning the rhyme and the reason
where there used to be no way.
Just watch and see
for these guys will be men someday.

Men

Potential unfolding, becoming real
finally deciphering how they feel.
No longer hiding from what we call life.
Embracing it, encasing it in the eyes of their wife.
Making commitments and planning their days,
learning the motives behind all their ways.
Seeking meaning beyond watching sports
finding fulfillment in activities of all sorts.
Cracking the cages, which hold off their hearts.
Learning how to love (or at least making a good start).
Looking behind them at all the bridges they have burned.
Reaching their destination and knowing there's much more to learn.

I watched a couple walk out of Borders tonight and I saw as
he slowly ran his hand up and down her back then led her
out of the store with his fingertips resting on her lower back.
That is what I want. That tender touch that so gently says
"I care."

Memorial Day

Marc and Lynda Unger called to say that they would be attending the service at the cemetery. I cautioned them that it might be very hard for them but they said someone had told them they would be speaking about Daniel. I said I would meet them there.

Kristen, Sam, and I went early and saved seats for them. Marc sobbed through most of the ceremony. Lynda and their three teenagers fought to hold back tears.

As I gazed over to Rebekah's gravesite, I knew that I needed to hold on to me and not get lost in sorrow. I needed to keep a clear head in order to help our dear friends.

I thought about how I had wondered what Marc's email announcement would be about Daniel's death. It was easy for him to quote Psalms 116:15 to me when it was Rebekah, but what would he say about his own son? But there it had been, in his own personal grief-stricken e-mail. "Precious in the sight of the Lord is the death of His godly ones". My friend proved what a man of integrity he is. The shock of the loss shivers everything within us, but Marc's trust in God was unshakeable.

I realized the helplessness of loving people so much and wanting to help, wanting to know just what to say.

> Find me words...powerful words
> > Words that speak peace to a broken heart
> Words that form a tourniquet where a hemorrhage flows
>
> Find me words...fragrant words
> > Words that drive the stench of death from horrified nostrils
> Words that bring healing sunlight in the midst of deepest darkness
>
> Find me words...joyous words
> > Words that bring laughter instead of weeping
> Words that produce smiles on grief-stricken faces
>
> Find me words...tender words
> > Words that cushion a savage blow
> Words that caress and embrace the punished, racing mind

Find me words...energizing words
>Words that will restore drained and ravaged bodies
Words that inject life when death tugs at the soul like quicksand

Find me words...encouraging words
>Words that flit like butterflies with beauty
Words that sparkle and enchant like fireflies in the twilight

Find me words...any kind of words
>Words that can stop the flow of tears
Words that can silence the inner wail of a shattered heart

Yet in the silence, I know...
There are no words...
>so God be near

Help me share with sorrowing tear
Let my heart be broken too
>so I can bear this sorrow with you

We went to lunch afterwards and Marc, who had not eaten a meal that he could remember, was able to enjoy the food and talk. He ended up falling asleep while still seated in the captain's chair after the meal.

"He is exhausted," Lynda confided. "He is going to preach at Daniel's service and has been arranging it all."

I wondered how in the world that he would be able to compose himself enough to preach his own son's funeral.

After a brief cat-nap, he shook himself awake and asked if I would help Lynda find something that she could wear to the funeral. Kristen and I took Lynda to JC Penney and I installed Lynda in the dressing room and then walked among the clothes racks to bring back some options. She was exhausted physically, but drained even more emotionally, so I wanted her to be able to relax while I looked. She tried on some different outfits and found a blue pantsuit that would work fine. We were able to go and make the purchase and get her out of the store and on her way home before she reached the melt-down point of exhaustion.

Walking into the Sistine Chapel, I could hardly contain myself. I kept seeing signs for it and wanted to run there, but I patiently waited to see it until we had slowly gone through every room. When we got there, I just sat and stared up at the ceiling in awe. I had wanted to go there my entire life, and I was finally there! It was larger than life and more beautiful than I could imagine. The Last Judgment was amazing. I had never noticed the part where someone's flesh is being pulled off and releasing their soul. It was amazing! I couldn't take my eyes off of the Creation of Man scene for the longest time. There is electricity flowing between God and Adam's fingers. It can't be mistaken.

Finally, I pulled myself away so we could go into St. Peter's.

We went up into the dome in St Peter's. It was amazing up there to be so close to the mosaics and also be able to look down into the cathedral, which is so huge. It really gives you perspective. We then went down and walked all around. Standing in front of the Pieta was so amazing. I never had dreamed that I would be there, staring at it. Jackie and I spent quite a bit of time walking around and looking at all the paintings and sculptures. They are all so complex in their own way. We saw everything in St. Peter's since we might not ever be back. It was an amazing day!

Funeral

What a whirlwind we experienced...from wedding to funeral in a few days. Caleb went with Sam, Kristen, and I to Daniel's service. Dressed in his Sheriff's department uniform, he sat, grim and saddened as Marc Unger spoke of his son's last moments. His duty had been to guard some Iraqi civilians who were providing services at their forward operating base. A mortar attack began and Daniel, who had been a speedy runner in track and baseball, made sure that the Iraqi civilians made it safely into the bunker in front of him. He saved their lives at the loss of his own. There were commendations from commanders and medals awarded. Marc spoke of his faith that he would see Daniel again. It was a very moving service.

The cemetery service was a full military burial. Marc had asked Sam if he would blow taps (since he is lead trumpeter with the CA National Guard), but Sam told him he did not think he could. He felt it would be too overwhelming. So another trumpet player from northern California blew taps and the twenty-one gun salute resounded and a weeping Lynda received the flag.

We went back home and tried to make plans for the rest of Kristen's time to have some fun and light-hearted activities since she had landed in the middle of what became crushing sorrow and loss. She had come for a wedding and partying down. She had been pressed into the middle of that joy but also the need of a grieving family who reached out for support as well.

We tried to soak up every moment of time before Kristen had to return home and then we were back to just the two of us in our home.

My weekend was filled with spending as much time as I possibly could with the people here that I love so dearly. I will miss them all. Only a fortnight left here in jolly ol' England and I will be home. Last night I was dreaming about home so vividly that when I woke up I was afraid to open my eyes because I truly believed that England had just been a dream and it was over now. It's sad because part of me wishes I had never come because good-byes and moving on are so very painful. From being here, I know that I never want to live a "normal life." I know that I will never be content staying in one place my whole life. I need to move. I need to experience. I need to fall in love with every bit of the world and have it fall in love with me too.

Yesterday afternoon was filled with playing tackle (American) football and ultimate Frisbee. We jumped on each other and ran and screamed, acting like little kids. It was so much fun. I loved every minute of it. Today we are going out to a proper Sunday dinner (lunch) at the Norwood. I will get to have Yorkshire pudding and all that fun stuff. Yet, all I keep thinking is "No! Make time stop." I am just finally getting to know everyone well. We are just finally getting close and loving each other heaps and I only have a fortnight to spend with them.

Time is a funny thing. When I think about home, it feels like I have been gone a really long time. When I just think about England and my experiences here it feels like I haven't even been gone a week. I still remember my first day here so vividly. I was completely jet lagged and just not feeling that well. We were walking up to the villas to pick where we were going to live. We were all still so confused and so unsure. Now, I walk towards my villa and realize that I know every little bump in the walkway. I know where everyone lives and all the door codes. I know the best people to go to for a cup of tea and chat.

England is a home to me. I'm trying to remember that when I go, everything will change. Everyone is moving out and on, not just me, not just the American students. None of the students that were in the halls this year will be there next year, they are all getting their own places to live. All the seniors I love are graduating. It will be different. Maybe I wouldn't love it as much next year. Life here would be different. So I will be content knowing that I had a four and a half month love affair with England and that it has changed me, deep down inside and I will never be the same again.

P.S. Response from Mom:

You are an amazing young woman who can take a totally foreign place and make it home. You can take complete strangers and make them dear friends. You can take common circumstances and make them eternal memories. You bring your "pixie dust" magic to any occasion and any setting and wherever you are, it is a better place for it.

46

Writing Contest

Summer arrived and with it the annual *What I Love About America* writing contest at Mineral King School. I came up with it after 9/11. It seemed everyone wanted to talk about what was wrong with us, why we deserved the shocking murder that took place on that day. So I wanted to land a counter-punch and get little minds thinking about what is so very wonderful about our nation.

For the past two years, Rebekah and I had collected the stories and adjourned to her room with them. Then, we would read them to one another. Laughter and tears were the order of the day as she helped me narrow the field down to five finalists in the upper (4th–6th grades) and lower (1st–3rd grade) divisions. The stakes were high because the third place winner in each division won $50, second place $75, and first place $100. I had a team of four other judges who helped select the winners and then Rebekah would accompany me to the awards ceremony as we handed out the cash and had the winners read their essays.

Rebekah had been so inspired that she had talked about writing a book about people who had come to this country and their views of how extraordinary and wonderful our freedoms are.

Well, it was time to collect the stories once again and go through the elimination process. I took them all upstairs and sat on Rebekah's bed and began reading through them. I made it through a few but then gathered them all up and went downstairs.

Sam was watching the news and I stood in front of the TV and announced, "I am going to need your help."

"Okay," he said.

I plopped down on the floor and divided the stack in two. "You read one and then I will read one," I instructed.

And he did. We talked and laughed and discussed and he helped me whittle the stories down to five finalists in each division. I had the judges come in and they voted and I was able to get all of the certificates prepared and the prize money attached to the winning essays. The day of the assembly, I packed all of the items up and left to go to the school.

As I climbed the stage to sit alone to be announced and to hand out the awards, I was feeling such a cramp of sadness. This has been one of those delicious moments that Rebekah and I shared. The children's faces, the back stories behind their essays, we loved it all.

Just then I looked to see a tall man walking across the platform to join me. It was Caleb, in his uniform. He had a gentle smile on his face as he approached. He is 6'2" and, in his all-black Sheriff's gear is a pretty imposing figure. My heart melted when he slid onto a chair next to me. He had requested, and had been granted, permission to attend the ceremony with me.

The school principal, who is a dear friend, pulled one of the crisp $100 bills out of the envelope when he was announcing that we would be handing out the awards. He said, "Hmmmm, I would like $100," and acted like he would pocket it.

He glanced back at Caleb who was waggling his finger back and forth in warning.

The principal acted scared and said, "Oh, she brought HIM along!" and the students exploded with laughter.

Caleb came and stood beside me as the students were called up to accept their awards. He shook each hand, told them "Congratulations!" and passed out the envelopes with the cash. My own personal security guard.

Thank you God for a son who knows where rough patches lie, and who comes alongside to help and support.

✆ *Rebekah's Journal* ✆

If you could go back in time and change one thing what would you change (in your life or in someone else's)?

If I could change one thing, I would really experience each moment in time. I wouldn't just live it. Anyone can live life... I mean we all breathe oxygen in and out and when that stops we die. But I would want to feel every single moment that I have been blessed to live. My mom says that out of all the people in the world, I am one of the few that really experience every moment, yet I still feel that I could experience it more. I want to notice everything. That's what I would change.

Family Reunion

Our family has had a reunion every other year since the late 70s. Dad felt it was important to make sure we stayed connected and so he rents the camp that I went to as a kid, Nebraska Youth Camp just south of Kearney, Nebraska and we all head out there for a week in August.

Rebekah and I canoeing on the lake at Nebraska Youth camp.

The head guy counselor - Harold - and the head girl counselor - Dena - when I was a kid, grew up and got married and now come and cook for us all.

We spend our days swimming and canoeing, hiking or just hanging out. There is lots of sand down by the lake for the little kids to play in. When the river is running high, Harold will load up the back of the flat bed trailer with inner tubes, hook up the tractor, and haul us all down to the bridge and we can spend a lazy afternoon tubing down the Platte. If there is time, and the water is running fast enough, he will pick us up and let us do it again before dinner.

All meals are held in the mess hall, but there are usually groups of people in there all day, playing board games or cards, piecing together a jigsaw puzzle, or making crafts. There is always something to do and someone to talk to.

When the children were younger, we used to drive out, exploring all of the sights in between. We had visited every national park west of Nebraska and had explored lots of roads between here and there over the years. We had hiked Zion National Park up to the Emerald Pools and discovered a little restaurant called Cactus Cowboy that made the best burger ever, we stood on the continental divide, picnicked at Custer National Park while watching herds of buffalo graze on the wind-swept hills around us. We stayed at the historic Irma Hotel in Cody, Wyoming and spent days enjoying the wonders and diversity of Yellowstone. Once the kids got older and time constraints began to impose, we took to flying and we had not really been on a great Western Adventure by car since 1994. I had kept meticulous records of each day and Rebekah was hoping she and Caleb and I could perhaps recreate that glorious time of adventure a decade later.

It was not to be.

Caleb could not get time off from his new job with the Sheriff's department so Sam and I invited Sara to join us and we flew into Kearney.

It had been twelve years since Sara had been to a reunion.

She was overjoyed with the chance to see and hug and talk to family from all across the country.

It had been years since Sam had attended as well. The camp does not have the most modern facilities and the Nebraska heat and humidity could really get to him so it had been the norm for it to be Caleb, Rebekah and I representing at the bi-annual gatherings. When Caleb was in the Marine Corps, it whittled down to just Rebekah and I as traveling and bunk buddies.

Now, I was back.

I walked down to the lake when we arrived and sat in one of the swings, looking out at the cottonwood rimmed, rippling water.

I love the camp. It has a deep, rich, full connection that I feel when I can smell the delicate aroma of plant and tree and water that makes up the essence of camp. I inhaled deeply, closing my eyes and letting the sun-sparkle through the trees warm my face.

The last reunion, Caleb and Rebekah and I had flown out together. We did not get in until well after dark. We put our stuff in our cabin and then found one of the large swings (like a porch swing mounted on metal frames) and scooched in together. As we looked up at the twinkling stars and were so thankful to be back, Caleb and I continued to push us higher and higher in the swing. Rebekah remarked, "I don't think we are supposed to swing this thing quite this high" when it happened. Her end of the swing slipped its S bolt and crashed to the ground and Caleb and I landed on her in a pile. We thought we had really done it, breaking the swing, but we hadn't and we could get it connected back again but poor Rebekah sported a bruise on her arm, black and blue, where we had squashed her. She told any ear that would listen, "And I was the one saying I did not think we should be doing it!" She loved to rib us about that, repeating her warning anytime we were up to something she did not think was so wise.

While at camp, Rebekah stayed up late and got up early, refusing to miss out on any adventure or chance to talk with beloved grandparents, aunts, uncles, cousins, and now her cousin's children. She helped the little ones roast marshmallows for S'Mores and would make sure they got their meals as she took them through the buffet line. She helped with crafts and sang songs and told stories. The two of us would start most mornings before sunrise out on the water in a canoe and rejoice as the sun made a diamond path across the lake. Often there would be deer that had come down to drink and fish jumping in the pre-dawn morn.

Looking out at the dazzling water, it felt as if I could reach out and touch Rebekah. It was one of those moments that I had come to refer to as Raspberry Perfume. When she was staying at home during winter break, there would be times when I would come home from the office and I could tell that she had just left for her job at Borders. She wore Raspberry Perfume and it would be lingering in the air so I knew she had just passed that way. That is how being back at camp made me feel and I treasured the chance to just be still and listen for the lingering echoes.

Like the last time we were there. Some of the cousin's children had rifled through our things in our cabin. Caleb, Rebekah, and I went looking for them and finally got a confession out of the culprits. Rebekah had looked at the son of a beloved cousin and said, "I'm not going to tell your parents."

He looked at her with such relief and joy as he heaved an audible sigh. But then she followed with a very stern and forceful command, "YOU are!"

He fell apart and literally required our assistance to locomote himself to the mess hall and his appointment with fate. There was much weeping and wailing and gnashing of teeth once the truth was told. I chuckled as I remembered Rebekah's face and her voice. She was kind and good and caring and soothing but a very righteous and fearsome avenger as well.

It was very tender seeing nieces who had loved Rebekah so. We had a chapel service and my oldest brother stood and spoke about how he just had to acknowledge the sadness of not having Rebekah among us. I stood and spoke about how she loved them all so much, and of course, we miss her desperately, but that it was the way she LIVED that we all need to remember. Each day, each moment, was a treasure to her. She didn't waste a one.

Then my brother led us in a hymn:

> *And He walks with me and He talks with me, and He tells me I am His own.*
> *And the joy we share as we tarry there, none other has ever known.*

I could see my niece Wendy, her cheek in profile, glistening with tears. Wendy, who had told Rebekah, "When God made you, He used only sugar!" Just thinking about that sweet compliment made Rebekah wiggle with joy!

I lost it. I did the ugly cry when you can't make your face behave and it has a mind of its own. I put my face in my hands and just let myself weep.

The time in Nebraska was good for me. I still found the sun in the morning in a canoe out on the lake. As I swam in its waters, I remembered all of the laughter and joy that echoed here and gently, gently it washed over me.

It was sweet to be with family, to laugh and play and reconnect.

As we got ready to leave (Sara, Sam and I) and were boarding our flight, I remembered a similar trio (Caleb, Rebekah, and I) two years ago.

Two years ago, we had been the sole remainders of out of state family at the camp on the last day.

As I was walking to the mess hall to get the coffee started, Dad called from behind me. I waited up for him and he said, "I thought I lost her!" in a dazed way.

"Who, Dad?" I asked.

"Mom," he replied. "I really thought I had lost her."

I slid my arm through his and asked him to tell me what had happened. While he was in the shower, Mom had come to the door, her face turning blue, trying to let Dad know she could not breathe. He tried doing a Heimlich maneuver but he was so slippery, he could not get a good grip so he laid her on the floor and managed to dislodge the prune that had been blocking her airway. Somehow she had swallowed it down the wrong pipe and could not breathe until Dad stuck his fingers down her throat and cleared it.

Dad was visibly shaken as he recounted the tale to me.

"I hollered," he said. "But no one came to help."

"I thought I heard something from my cabin," I admitted, "but when I stopped and listened, I didn't hear any more".

Dad looked up at me and gave a half-hearted chuckle. "Prob'ly a good thing you didn't come," he said. "Neither of us being dressed and all."

I nodding, smiling back into his eyes and stroking his hand. No need for long-term therapy. Thank you, God!

Dad hesitated for a moment. "Go and make sure she's okay," he pleaded.

I walked back to their cabin and gently knocked on the door. "Mom...are you doing okay?"

Her voice came back, scratchy and weak. "I'm alright," she assured. "I'll be along in a minute."

I rejoined Dad on the path and we walked, arm in arm, to the mess hall and put the coffee on to brew. By the time we were pouring steaming mugs for ourselves, Mom and Caleb and Rebekah had shown up. We filled our plates with breakfast waffles and strawberries and eggs and sausage and while we ate our meal, Mom and Dad retold the story for Caleb and Rebekah.

Making S'mores around the camp fire at our family reunion. Rebekah is on the far right.

Rebekah's brow was furrowed with concern and she continually rubbed her hand over Grandma's shoulders and squeezed her grandpa's hand reassuringly.

"I'm just glad that I wasn't the camp's first casualty," Mom said.

"No more prunes before breakfast," Rebekah said and everyone laughed.

Mom and Dad took us to the Kearney airport and waited with us for the plane to arrive. They would not drive away until they had seen us safely into the sky. The small plane arrived and they checked us through and we climbed aboard. The plane was so small that there was only one seat on either side of the aisle. I sat across the aisle from Rebekah and Caleb sat behind her. We could

In this photo, our family is playing cards together. Rebekah's grandpa has his back to the camera. Rona's brother Rod is to his left and then Rebekah's grandma is sitting in back (upper left). Rona and her sister, Judie, are sitting at the upper right, and Rebekah is just to grandpa's right.

see Mom and Dad standing at the plate glass window in the airport. They were waving their hands to us and Rebekah leaned closer to the window and waved and waved and waved as the plane began its taxi. She waved until the terminal disappeared behind us and then she leaned her head back in the seat and cried in anguish, "Oh, will I ever see them again?"

Mom's brush with death had made it so clear that we were approaching the time when the two year gaps in visits posed a bigger and bigger threat as to whether they would live for the next reunion.

Her cry was so heart-breaking that I had a mini-meltdown as well and Caleb was leaning forward trying to console his sis while she and I had a good cry.

Now, once again as I watched Mom and Dad standing at that same plate glass window in the terminal, their hands waving briskly to us as we waited to take off, I was struck by the profound depth of Rebekah's question. The answer was no, but I would have never thought that she would be the one who would not be back to our next reunion.

But there it was. The least expected absence of all.

And I realized once again how fragile life is, and how we can never assume how much time we have left.

∞ *Rebekah's Journal* ∞

The last place in my life I would want to see?

Nebraska. I am very rooted there and when I go "home" to NE my soul sings. I light up with the fireflies and am in love with life again.

Of all of the people that I would like to get to spend a day with, it would be my grandfather. I would want to spend the day with him because he and I are really close even though we don't see each other that much. He is also getting elderly and I am not sure how much longer he will be around.

I would sit and play cards with him all day because that is one of his favorite things to do and since he is getting older, he is not able to do the really active stuff much anymore without suffering a lot of pain. So we sit and talk and play cards. It's actually great fun. I miss my grandpa.

Election Season and See How They Run

Fall election season began in full swing and I organized the annual ***See How They Run*** event for high school seniors. It is an all-day, invitation-only session where four students from each of the local high schools come out.

In the morning, we have elected officials from city, county, state, and federal office who come in 30 minute segments and the students can ask questions and get a chance to actually have a conversation with them.

The afternoon is spent playing the game *See How They Run* which is like monopoly on steroids. The purpose of the game is to get students interested and connected to the political process.

Since we had been conducting the event for years, I have a system of contacting individuals at each high school and those in elected office and getting everything organized and underway as the school year kicks in.

Rebekah had become my right hand helper once she had graduated high school and had come to the ensuing events as a scorekeeper and assistant.

She was the kind of person that would always find the area that needed propped up or the task that needed to be done and then she would do it, quietly,

unobtrusively, and cheerfully. Having her present anywhere was a joy because she was such an eager participant, an intuitive helper, and a contributor in every way to the success of whatever was occurring.

So, it was another one of those gaping vacuum places that I could feel her absence in reminders that were painful and undeniable.

But I was learning, from the grit teeth resolve of refusing to turn aside from any event just because it might hurt, that once I stepped across the threshold and decided to participate, decided to proceed, I was also granted heavenly grace to accomplish what I had committed to.

You just have to keep going, keep fighting because it is the only thing that lets you know that you are still alive... when sometimes that does become a big question.

whether or not your heart keeps beating when all that seems to be there is a big void where it once beat. but I guess all you can do is hope for things to change and for things to get better...keep breathing. keep going...but I can't do what you asked and paste on a fake smile because sometimes you need to cry...tears can be so cleansing when you are hurting...

maybe it is time to just sit in the road of life for a while and let myself see who I am and what I need to be...I thought I knew for a while...

Thanksgiving

Thanksgiving is always a time of good food, fun, and fellowship. Mostly, it has been just our immediate family over the years. When Sam and I married, I instituted a tradition. In order to enjoy the meal, everyone had to arrive with a thankful list. It could be just one word, but it had to be on paper and in writing.

With all of the food served and waiting to be eaten, the steam rising from the dressing and mashed potatoes and the platter of turkey, we would read what we had written to one another. From the beginning, little Rebekah really put her heart and pen into expressions of gratitude. In her younger years, she would often appear with several pages for her Thankful List.

Over the years, she learned to be more concise in her offering of thanks, but her heart flowed very freely in Thanksgiving. One year, in addition to her list, she had made personalized cards for each one of us with our name making an acronym of the things she loved and treasured about us. The following year, there were name cards at each place setting and inside, written in a tracing of her hand were five things she loved and treasured about us.

Sam and I had been leading a small group Bible study for years. In fact, there had been a period of time when the only attendees were Sam and I and Rebekah (and Ginger our dog but she did not enter into the discussions). If no one else showed up, the three of us would go through the study and discussion questions provided by our pastor.

Once Rebekah started college, there were quite a few new people who began attending. One couple in particular never missed. They often needed a ride, assistance, or had other needs but they were always at small group Bible study. They had been hinting about having nowhere to go for Thanksgiving. Sam and I had discussed it. Caleb and Missy would be having Thanksgiving with her family. Sara was coming to our home and we would prepare a meal but I did not think I would be up to much hoopla. That was the plan and it sounded like a good one.

Then the Sunday before Thanksgiving, our pastor challenged us in his sermon. He challenged us to reach out, to share, to invite and welcome people into our lives. As I listened, I felt something melting in me and after the service I held Sam tight in a hug and told him, "It's okay. They can come over" as I watched the couple approaching behind him.

Sam shook hands and said, as if he had been planning it for ages, "We would love to have you join us for Thanksgiving" and so they did.

I got up early and pulled out all of the previous years' lists and read and re-read them in tears. Then I wrote my own and got busy cooking. Sara arrived and helped me get everything set up and soon our guests arrived and before I knew it, we were all gathered around the steaming platters and holding our thankful lists in front of us to share. With a little bit of shaky voices, Sam and Sara and I read our lists out and then we dug in to the meal. Sara helped me with the clean-up while the others adjourned to the living room. Sam offered to put a movie on and they were selecting one. I suggested to Sara that we take Ginger for a brief walk. We slipped out the front door and into the day. The sky was crystalline blue and the trees were losing their leaves. We made a game of picking up the maple leaves as we walked, trying to find the one leaf with the most colors on it.

Some had green, yellow, red, orange, even a deep purple as the turning moved from stem to leaf tip. So lovely, each one completely and totally unique.

Sara and I talked about the discomfort of having guests during such a tender time laced with memories, but how God had actually given us a gift, rare and sweet. Our escape from the house had become a treasure hunt of beauty and fellowship. Breathing the brisk November air, we both had to acknowledge that, in spite of the circumstances, in spite of our longing for Rebekah's presence and her gentle, thankful heart, we had tapped into the absolute flood of Thanksgiving from our own hearts that year and it had been a very good day.

Today, as I remember all that has happened over the past year, I realize how much there is to be thankful for.

I am thankful for my family and friends for all their support over the past years and believing in me even when I do not believe in myself!

I am thankful for all of the opportunities I have had and how much my eyes have been opened to the world and all of the possibilities that it holds.

As we near the end of this year, I look forward to the year to come and all of the wonders it will hold for all of us.

(Rebekah's Thankful List 2003)

Autumn Leaves

The autumn leaves fall to the ground
making intrinsic circles as they descend.
Their shadows cast a kaleidoscope pattern
against the parched grass.
People pass
by without noticing
nature's art taking place at their feet.
They stomp through the leaves hearing the crunch
as they disintegrate underfoot.
They seldom realize what they are doing.
Do people ever notice life as it is going by?
The beauty in the wind,
the falling of the leaves
as it all paints a picture
on the canvas of the world.

If Santa made grandparents,
he'd make them all like **YOU!**

Merry Christmas
with Lots of Love

You said you wanted grandbabies
right? Well here's a start. You guys
will make the best grandparents
ever. Love you bunches.
Caleb
Missy

The note on our christmas card from Caleb and Missy.

Christmas

Christmas is not a day in our family. It is an entire season.

And Rebekah was always my partner in turning our home into a showplace. We got the tree all strung with lights and put up the sweet and dear ornaments that we had collected over the years. Each one got attention and comment as we lovingly unwrapped them and selected the perfect spot on the tree.

The year before, as Rebekah was arranging the nativity scene with all of the trees and shepherds positioned just so, she suddenly sat back on her heels with a sharp intake of breath. "Mom," she cried. "I may not be here next year. Promise you will put everything up like we always do."

I smiled and laughed at her. She was making plans to pursue her Master's Degree in England, and she knew that she very well could be far from home so I agreed, and we shook on it – everything, just the same.

And I kept the promise, rising early and toting all of the containers into the living room. Just opening the lid made me ache. The last time they were out of their boxes, both of our hands were busy loving it all. Each ornament and bit of décor, each member of the nativity scene, had been exposed to the rare atmosphere of pure joy that was Rebekah's.

Christmas decorating. Now they had me, me, plodding along and doing my best to place and display and welcome in the season. And I did, stopping to enjoy a mug of coffee as I looked around the transformed room with a sense of melancholy joy.

I did our annual Christmas shopping for children of the community as well.

Each year, our church, in partnership with Visalia Unified School District provides Christmas for families who are selected by their teachers. We have a Christmas program in the evening, and then hand out the presents to the children and they take them home unwrapped for Christmas morning. We also make sure every family gets a box jam-packed full of food that will provide not only a Christmas feast but staples for the month.

While Rebekah lived, we never missed one together. The first one had us tending infants in the nursery while a group of several families enjoyed a meal and took home their gifts. The event had grown and this year there would be over 1200 children receiving a sweatshirt, sweatpants, new shoes, and a toy to take home.

My job assignment was to be a greeter and I was positioned outside the front doors of the sanctuary. It was a clear, crisp night and as I gazed up at the starry darkness, I felt so alone. My heart cried out, "Oh, Lord, I miss her so much! It's times like these that have been such sweet times together that it is hardest!"

I remembered the prior year, she had driven down from work at Borders in Fresno and she had on thick-soled white sneakers. I teased her that they looked like clown shoes and she leaped up and clicked her heels together and did a funny dance that had us all laughing.

As I stood in the silence, I once again lodged my protest to the heavens.

"Remember all of the plans we made, God? The things we were going to do with her precious babies?"

Silence was my only answer and I knew I needed to stop because soon people would be arriving and I would need to be warm and welcoming in my role as greeter.

But suddenly I felt the Lord speak to my heart. "Daughter, you have a choice. You can resent the fact that Rebekah is not here. You can let every memory remind you of loss...OR, I can show you a new way. You can be set utterly free and consider every child that walks the globe Rebekah's child!"

I let that sink in and said, "Lord, I choose to see them as Rebekah's children." A miracle occurred. No matter what shape those children arrived in for the event, if they had snot from here to their navel (and some of them did!) I quickly swept their face with a wipey (if they would let me) and welcomed them with JOY. God filled my heart to overflowing with His love for those kids and taught me a new truth. We really CAN choose His joy.

Christmas has its requirements, things that must happen, and I tried to do them all. I baked the cookies and decorated the home. I shopped for presents and tried to harness my focus on what would be pleasing and good for family and friends.

On Christmas Eve for years now, it had been a fun little thing to watch the *Muppet's Christmas Carol* together. When Caleb was in the Marine Corps, stationed in Okinawa, we missed him so very much as we sang along with the show. Now Sam, Caleb, Sara, and I huddled together to continue the tradition and watch it together. As the music began, I remembered Rebekah's joyful little squirmy dance and her exclamation, "After all, there's only one more sleep 'til Christmas!"

When the song *Bless Us All* began, Caleb was singing along, as best he could. I could not but was silently weeping as the beloved words filled the darkened room. Sam leaned over to me in tears as he whispered, "I can hear her voice!"

We made it through the movie, drained and red-eyed. We talked afterwards for a bit and then Caleb was on his way with the promise that he would be back the next day.

Christmas morning I got up early to make cinnamon rolls and get the ham in the oven. Soon the smell of rising bread and cinnamon sugar laced the air with goodness.

Sara, Caleb and Missy arrived and we exchanged presents and laughed and talked.

Then Caleb handed me a Christmas card. I looked at his face and he eagerly urged me to open it.

Inside it said – For Extra-Special Grandparents

"You said you wanted grandbabies, right? Well, here's a start. You guys will make the best grandparents ever. Love you bunches, Caleb and Missy

I read and re-read the writing, leaning over for Sam to read it too.

Caleb had retreated to sit on the couch with Missy and they were both beaming.

I stammered, "Really! REALLY!" and they both laughed and nodded. I jumped to my feet and hugged them both...and joyous conversation saturated the room.

Christmas! Christmas! That beloved promise of Hope and Light!

Simple Gift (Treasure Memories)

Treasure gift
given to me
from the depths
of your hearts.
It's not the value
that matters,
but the love
which you impart.
Giving to me
everything within you
with just one
price-tagged gift.
Yet, there is no price
that I would accept
for the love I feel from this.

Urgent Prayer

Take away the desires of my heart.
Mold them into Yours.
Burn away the passions that I feel.
Fan them into your flame.
Pry away all the wrong I have learned.
Teach me only Your truth.
Break away the calluses I have built.
Make my heart soft to Your work.
Tear away my worldly ways.
Let me live for no one, but You.

Yahrzeit

I wrote a letter to the local Christian radio station.

I just wanted to write and say how thankful I am for the ministry of KDUV.

The year 2004 has been the most challenging year of my life. On January 13th, our youngest daughter Rebekah, age 21, died in a single car accident that still remains a mystery to me. On her way home to her dorm room at Fresno Pacific University from her job at Borders bookstore, her car left the upper tier of the 180 connector and fell to the bridge midway down. The impact was so great that the car broke in two and the engine fell separately from the rest of the car body to Freeway 41 below. Rebekah was killed instantly, but no one else was harmed as the engine and car fell the additional 70 feet to a well-traveled roadway. It is miraculous that no others were harmed in any way.

The shock of her loss was so great and in the days and months that followed, I listened to KDUV whenever I could, sometimes lying on her bed and just weeping as I listened to "the message in the music".

Many songs blessed me. One song – *Will you be there?* – by Skillet, nearly killed me as its lyrics described exactly what my mind's eye pictured...when I'm falling down... as my heart grows cold...because my Mommy's heart grieved when I thought of Rebekah dying alone and yet, through that song my heart shouted over and over that... Yes, He was there and Rebekah was not alone when she passed from this life to eternity.

You see, she and I were avid KDUV listeners and often, we would turn up the volume and belt out the songs as we drove around together on errands. I can remember her sweet face, with tears streaming down as we would sing – *I Can Only Imagine* by Mercy Me or her funny "dance moves" to Switchfoot's *Gone*. Those memories of the shared music and the conversations that they inspired have been such a blessing to me.

I miss Rebekah, probably always will while I live on this earth, but I want you to know that while she lived we both benefited from your ministry and now that she has departed and I remain, you have comforted and encouraged, blessed and inspired me to continue to hold tight to God's hand and seek first His kingdom.

THANK YOU for your holy ministry and may God continue to encourage and bless your efforts,

Rona Swanson

And I sent an e-mail out to friends:

J. M. Barrie, the playwright who gave us Peter Pan wrote, "God gave us memories so that we might have roses in December."

Today I am so thankful for memory and the sweet moments of love and tenderness that I can recall whenever I wish. Isn't it wonderful that we are so blessed that even in the winter times of ordinary and dreary days such blossoms can open and come to life for us, reminding us of the eternal nature of God's goodness?

We have a rose bush in our back yard. The kids always called it the Sleeping Beauty bush because of its long thorns but it has the most fragrant pink blooms. Sunday January 11, 2004 (her last day at home) Rebekah and I were sitting in the living room and she looked out the window. The Sleeping Beauty was awake and covered with pink blossoms.

"Roses don't bloom in the winter!" Rebekah exclaimed.

I joined her and laughed. "They're blooming for you!" I said. And so they were.

I pray that you have roses in December and that your coming year is blanketed in God's petals of blessing and joy.

The year has ended and a new year begun.

It feels like a drum beat, booming deeper and deeper as the day approaches.

A dear friend sent flowers to Sam and to me.

My card says "Dear Rona, We wanted to send you love as you get through this week."

Oh, that the love of friends could be a puncture-proof barrier for the pain of remembrance.

It is a strange thing to try and hold tenderly the memories of a dear one and not be wounded by the sharp sense of loss. A two-edged sword indeed.

But the day, January 13th, arrives.

I try to conduct myself as if it is any other day but it isn't, it isn't.

My heart knows the ground we are treading and its significance.

Jewish tradition calls it a yahrzeit. It is a remembrance and the one year mark as the calendar has come around again to the fateful day.

I am still breathing.

I go to work.

The activity distracts and holds my focus.

I eat a meal.

I pass the time.

I go home.

I get ready for bed.

But I cannot sleep.

Instead, I lay in bed, reading my Bible.

The clock is nearing that time — the time when one year ago, on a darkened freeway, my daughter left this world and stepped into eternity.

My heart pounds as if it is happening right now, this moment.

Every nerve inside me is singing and I want to scream out a warning, make a call, and send some help.

But of course, I know it is futile.

It is done.

It is past.

But still I lie in bed, wide awake.

Finally, I look at my dear husband who is reading quietly nearby.

"I don't know what I am waiting for," I confess. "The phone call at 2:30? An officer at our door?"

He smiles gently, holding out his hand.

I get up.

I put on a CD and climbed back under the covers.

Untitled Hymn by Chris Rice came on.

I let the music wash over me as wave upon wave of tears poured down. I lay down on my side, drawing my legs tight against my chest. Sam bent over me... wanting to comfort.

As the music continued, I pictured Rebekah, dancing with abandon and joy

Then the final verse began...

> *And with your final heartbeat*
> *Kiss the world goodbye*
> *Then go in peace, and laugh on Glory's side, and*
> *Fly to Jesus*
> *Fly to Jesus*
> *Fly to Jesus and live!*

I sang along, with all of my heart— "Fly to Jesus, Fly to Jesus, Fly to Jesus and LIVE!"

I was sobbing as I lifted my arms and belted out the final refrain.

I had a good cry and felt something let loose within me...a release...a surrender.

"God," I prayed. "Thank you for Rebekah. Thank you that she is safe home. Thank you that I will never witness another tear in her eye, that she is completely and fully consumed by joy. and thank you for keeping us and sustaining us and helping us through this past year. May we never let go of your good hand."

∞ *Rebekah's Journal* ∞

Soar Away

Spinning beneath the stars with you
I let my spirit soar
Every burden flies away
And I am left
Here in your arms

Let Your Light Shine

sometimes I am afraid
to let my light shine
because I don't think
it is bright enough.

But, if I just hide my light,
however big or small it is,
I am doing nothing
for the one who gave it to me.

By covering my light
I am saying I am ashamed
of the gift He gave me
and of His workmanship.

He gave us all the light of the world
and put it deep within.
Don't be afraid to let it shine in all you do
and He will shine through you.

Where Do We Go From Here?

It is a funny thing about grief. You can think you are doing so well, and then something can come out of left field and flatten you again.

We are never "safe" from sorrow if we leave our hearts open.

Those who have experienced extreme loss and pain may want to close every door, shutter every entrance to their heart, but that is an early entry into a self-made tomb.

But to leave the entries open leaves us completely vulnerable to pain.

The year Rebekah died was a record year of rain in the Mojave Desert. The following spring botanists flocked to the desert to see what had not been seen in decades. Flowers blanketed the desert floor, rare blooms that had lain dormant until the flood of rainwater that had fallen coaxed them awake. A friend traveled there and brought back photos of the miraculous blooms.

And I wondered if in the same way, the floods to my very soul would yield rare and unique blossoms as well.

I read this portion of scripture...

> [5] Blessed are those whose strength is in you,
> who have set their hearts on pilgrimage.
> [6] As they pass through the Valley of Baca,
> they make it a place of springs;
> the autumn rains also cover it with pools.
> [7] They go from strength to strength,
> till each appears before God in Zion.
>
> – Psalm 84:5-7 (NIV)

In a recent Psalms study this passage was pointed out and the Valley of Baca was explained as a place of tears, well actually a hollow of sorrow, a place of weeping, but the kind of grief that is the vomit of crying. If this anguish hits you, it is coming OUT! It is the leveling of all of your dignity and control in the heart-breaking, gut-wrenching, unintelligible, yet universally understood sound of a human being at their lowest.

I know that place.

I have been there.

There are places in our lives that feel as if they can swallow us.

Deep dark depressions that wrap their velvety claws about us.

We need to remember that this is not our home.

We are only pilgrims here, headed for our forever country.

Since you have made it this far with me, I want to encourage you to keep walking.

The road can be weary and rough at times, but God knows the path we take, and He will never leave us or forsake us.

Afterword

As the years have passed since those first dark days, I have witnessed God's ability to hold us together when it feels like everything is falling apart again and again. I have discovered that the life of a believer in a Mighty Redeemer is an adventure, not for the faint of heart, but that He is also the One who reminds us "Fear not!"

Our first little granddaughter arrived August 17th, 2005 and Caleb and Missy named her Rebekah Faith. What a joy she is to all of us! She has been joined by Emma Grace and Arabelle Marie and our home rings with laughter and song and play. Rebekah's former bedroom now houses Lucky the amazing spring-horse, who whinnies and neighs and does all kinds of great things as they ride the range. There are many other toys and games and books and instruments to play. It is my granddaughter's private world of fun and imagination. Who knows, there may be more to follow, and we will joyously embrace any new siblings as well!

I had a dream the other day, a dream where Rebekah and I were folding laundry together. There was a big pile of clean clothes and we were down on the floor in the living room, just folding clothes and chatting quietly. She would chuckle and comment and then I would answer. It was gentle and calm and lovely. It was so very, very ordinary. When I woke up, I wanted to dial up that dream again and fold the whole world's laundry, but that did not work for me.

There was no going back.

Do I miss her? Oh, more...more than can be measured.

But I have learned to stand in awe of the treasure of her life, the depth of her love and selflessness and her willingness to live, truly live in each day, embracing it fully and squeezing every drop of joy out of it.

May you be challenged to not let another day slip by thoughtlessly or heartlessly.

I found a copy of an old e-mail from me to Rebekah:

Dear Beck,

Have you thought about what a hand-hold means? I was just thinking about how I would like to be able to hold your hand and tell you that I love you and I am praying for you. As your last week of this school year passes, I know that you will have tremendous up and down emotions. Anyway, I got to thinking about the word hand-hold and how important, in touchy situations, a place to hold on to can be to keep us from tumbling down or losing our balance. I am longing for the Lord to always be a handhold for me, when I feel insecure or I am reaching for a new altitude. I am so thankful that our Father graciously reaches out to us and steadies our wobbly legs. I promise He will steady any knocking knees that you might have for finals and give you hand-holds that won't give way.

I love you,
Mom

Oh, how I have learned how sure and steady God's hand is when everything else seems to be crumbling.

Psalms 46

[1] God is our refuge and strength,
 an ever-present help in trouble.
[2] Therefore we will not fear, though the earth give way
 and the mountains fall into the heart of the sea,
[3] though its waters roar and foam
 and the mountains quake with their surging.

It is my prayer that you will clasp the hand-hold of heaven held out to you. May your ordinary day become Son-dazzled and brilliant, and you too can taste LOVE — more than can be measured!

Dear Rebekah,

Hope these wishes cheer you
and brighten your day—
remember that you're thought of
in the very fondest way.

I love you – more
than can ever be
measured,

Mom

Acknowledgements

First and foremost – it is with complete and utter adoration that I thank God for His love, His mercy, His grace and His determination to stay beside me when the world fell around me. Even as I felt like all of the stars had been commanded to crash down and that darkness would consume me, He was my light.

To my family – Sam, Sara, Caleb, and the throbbing loss we walked through together. We will not forget.

To Missy – my beloved daughter-in-law, thank you for your understanding.

To my granddaughters – Rebekah, Emma, and Arabelle. My cup overflows the moment I see you and hear your laughter.

To Mom and Dad – thank you for the love and support that has been bedrock in my life.

To my brothers and sister and extended family – thank you for your love and support. It sustains me still. I am so blessed to be so enfolded in your gentle love.

To Jimmy, Jen, Jackie, and all of Rebekah's FPU family – I love you, always and forever.

To Diana – who brought the essentials – bread, butter, paper plates and toilet paper to our home. Thank you for your sensible provision and your fierce love for our Rebekah.

To the sweet and gentle friends who came beside us. Sam and I referred to you all as life-savers. Not the sweet candy with the hole in the middle but the actual buoys thrown to the drowning who are caught in a wild and angry sea. You came to us and let us hang on, catch our breath, and survive the storm. I have learned to say, "How do you know who your real friends are? They are the ones who have had your tears and snot on their shoulder, and kept hanging on!" You have seen us at our worst and we will never forget your kindnesses and expressions of love and sympathy to us.

To my nagger-in-chief – ***Vickie*** – who believed in me when I did not believe in myself and hounded me to write this down.

To Alex – who read each iteration and who confessed that he would love to hear Rebekah's voice more often. He set me free to have her voice in each and every chapter.

To Chuck – dear friend, gentle giant, musician whose strains of *Fairest Lord Jesus/Jesu, Joy of Man's Desiring* will forever awaken a swirling mix of love and sorrow in me. Thank you for lovingly matching photos and illustrations to this work. It is so much better because you have touched it.

To Rebekah – for all of the joy and love...and for the reunion yet to come.